MYSTICAL REASON

MYSTICAL REASON

William Earle

REGNERY GATEWAY, INC.
CHICAGO

Copyright © 1980 by William Earle
Published by Regnery Gateway, Inc., Book Publishers
116 South Michigan Avenue, Chicago, Ill. 60603

Manufactured in the United States of America

Library of Congress Catalog Card Numbrs: 79-92079
International Standard Book Number: 0-89526-677-6

Library of Congress Cataloging in Publication Data

Earle, William, 1919-
  Mystical Reason.

  1. Soul.   2. God.   3. Identity.   4. Reason.
5. Phenomenology.   I. Title
BD423.E2   212   79-92079
ISBN 0-89526-677-6

To:

Corban LePell

Contents

Preface

It is a pleasure to acknowledge support from both the College of Arts and Sciences and the Graduate School of Northwestern University, which have been generous in their grants for my work. Mrs. Audrey Thiel and Linda Patrik have been responsible not merely for typing the manuscript but in improving some awkward sentences. To both, my deepest thanks.

Other friends have, without in the least agreeing with it, nevertheless supported me in the project, and I am most grateful to them: Professor John N. Findlay has kept a friendly but suspicious eye on some aspects of it, and then professors Tom Mueller, Donald Morano, Joseph Galloway, William Fowkes, William Langan, Errol Harris, and my colleague Professor Philip Grier have gone so far as to positively encourage it.

The two versions of the Ontological Argument in Spinoza are reprinted from *Spinoza, A Collection of Critical Essays* (Anchor Books, Doubleday, 1973), editor: Marjorie Grene.

My warmest thanks to all these and others, and of course it goes without saying that I alone am responsible for its deficiencies.

W.E.

Introduction

Mystical reason might, at first glance, seem to be a contradiction in terms; indeed, are mysticism and reason not two of the most ancient enemies? And, understood in a superficial way, they remain so. But part of the purpose of this book is to show progressively that a deeper and more ancient understanding of what they both are removes the hostility between them. Mysticism is not in the least an affair of irrational swooning, visions, and ecstacies, nor is reason an affair of drawing out long chains of argumentations about increasingly empty abstractions. Mysticism certainly loves its visions, and reason also exhibits itself in analysis, refutations, and formal deductions, and no doubt both have their peculiar functions and virtues. But that either should imagine these secondary phenomena to be its own very essence is a preliminary error which can be removed; mysticism deepens itself into an intuited identity of the self of the mystic and God, and reason plumbs itself into its own rational intuition of the identity of the *transcendental ego* which exercises reason, and *absolute reality* of which the transcendental ego is the consciousness.

Both of these claims amount to one; the languages alone differ. Both rest upon intuition, upon the immediate apprehension by the self both of itself and God. Since the core of the matter lies in intuition, and not inference, the claims of intuition must be looked into. Is not intuition locked within itself, forever condemned to inspecting the figments or phenomena of its own mind and imagination? How can it verify a claim to the objectivity of its object without in fact leaving itself, in order to conduct a second intuition of the "real" object lying outside itself, comparing that object with its former intuited object, to see whether in fact they are the same or different? But any such project is, on the face of it, futile, and therefore some have felt it necessary to bolster up their initial intuitions with "faith," "belief," "the concurrence of others" or assumptions about their practical utility. And sometimes popular science is trotted out to show that at least it has no basic objections.

That the validation of the claims of both mystical and rational intuition requires no such thing, and indeed renders it preposterous, can be seen from what is now called "pure phenomenology" or what used to be called "rationalism" in forms developed by Descartes, Spinoza, and Leibniz, among others. There, "clear and distinct" or "adequate" ideas were shown to be not merely sufficient unto themselves, but the very criteria for any other sort of lower-grade truth. The first chapter, "Ode to Phenomenology," tries to make evident that consciousness can indeed grasp immediately or intuitively its proper objects, objects which are objectively just as they present themselves to consciousness. In a word, that the mind has neither any possibility of departing from its own nature as mind in order to ascertain whether its objects are "real" or not; nor is there, of course, any need of its doing so. The fear of solipsism, or of being caught in a theater of my own inventions, is groundless and, worse, philosophically absurd.

The fear would never have arisen in the first place, however, if it were seen that all the objects of consciousness are not alike. Some indeed do have a merely phenomenal or fantastic being; my dream world, my imaginations, my sensations do not all represent things in an external world. But then, the God of the mystics and the *absolute reality* of the philosophers, taken here as the same, have, in and of their own nature, nothing whatsoever in common with imaginations, dreams, sensory perceptions. They of themselves declare their profound and radical difference of essence from such things. A following chapter then explores the given meaning or sense of what is intuited as absolute reality. And so, within the phenomenological scene, something is given as an object, which must necessarily be, and be in its own unique way. Traditionally, and here also, the determination of such an object and the defense of it as an infinite and necessary *being* is called the "ontological argument." It rests entirely upon recovering the sense of what is given phenomenologically to intuitive reason: and while in some forms it is presented as a maze of arguments, in effect that argumentation has the point only of removing misunderstandings and objections, all of which are based upon an inattention to the essence of what is given to either intuitive reason or mystic experience. As argumentation, it is a *via negativa:* as intuition, it is not argument but self-evidence.

A fourth chapter looks at that self or transcendental ego to which, or whom, the phenomenon of the *absolute* is given. It is not the self as the animating soul of the body, nor as citizen, husband, wife, agent in the world, nor an electrochemical phenomenon or epiphenomenon, nor indeed a temporal event in the world at all. It is of course related to these things, and is itself presupposed by any mundane act of consciousness, but the transcendental ego or self is precisely transcendental to these, not reducible to them, and, being neither born, living, nor dying, is eternally actual. That any such thing is true must offend every naturalist, pragmatist or materialist of whatever stamp; the transcendental ego is not accessible to their researches, can only be characterized by terms absurd in their own vocabularies, and from it no empirical consequences whatsoever can be deduced. But no matter, such considerations do not prevent its being, whereas other considerations detailed here do insist absolutely upon its being. Now this transcendental self, as will emerge, has, as its very essence, the same absolute or divine character elucidated in the earlier discussion. It is an identity with God, that is, God first taken objectively, now taken subjectively, or — put otherwise — the transcendental consciousness of absolute reality. Regarded as an individual, it is that absolute situated in the world for as long as it is: in itself, it is a point of their identity. Again, it is an ancient doctrine running from the Neo-Platonists, through medieval mystics such as Meister Eckhardt, through many, many others, Angelus Silesius, the Spanish mystics, etc., down through Descartes (a true but unlikely candidate), Spinoza, Leibniz, and — provisionally skipping Kant — through Hegel and many of our own contemporaries. My own discussion of the transcendental ego derives largely from Descartes' famous and disputed argument, "I think, therefore I am," as well as from Husserl. And therefore two arguments found in Descartes as well as others, the ontological argument and the *cogito ergo sum*, only slightly revamped in phenomenological terms, are found of course absolutely sound and of absolute importance to any philosophy not foundering in the finite things and hypotheses of scientific empiricism. That both have also been held to be highly questionable, when in point of fact they are both of absolute certitude, only shows the need for the work of comprehension rather than argumentation. Comprehension of the sense of what Descartes says in this domain requires a reenactment, by the reader, of the course of thought which ends in intuition. Descartes therefore calls one of his works *Meditations:* in it, the reader is not so much coerced to agree as invited to share reflections which will conduct him to his own indubitable intuitions.

A final chapter tries to bring these somewhat abstract considerations down to earth, without grounding them there. If a rationalistic or empirical philosophy dominates our times, and indeed probably most times, I shall argue that at least in

one famous old trio — the good, the beautiful, and the true —
any analysis whatsoever of these domains which does not
trace them back to the absolute self is not merely hopelessly
confused and embarked on a course of ratiocination which
can find no essential end but, put in more common terms,
simply blasphemous. That logic should be called "blasphemous" might startle some of our friends of formal logic. But
I hope enough will have been said in the previous sections to
make the allegation stick. And the same goes for an aesthetics
or ethics without God.

Alas, my own discussion is almost willy-nilly of an ex-
cessive abstraction. There is no help for it, and my apology
for its tediousness is by way of adding a miscellaneous collection of beautiful texts by those most usually thought of as
mystics. They were selected from a diversity of sources and,
while not altogether at random, at least with no systematic
purpose in mind.

An appendix includes matter not integral to the text, but
perhaps of some related interest to the reader.

Chapter I **Ode to Phenomenology**

Perhaps nothing could be more repellent than some objective manifestations of mystic experience. The eyes close or roll upwards or stare; the body may go rigid; there may be sweating or pallor, in any case a reduced metabolism; stigmata appear among Christians; speech may be in an unknown tongue, or in metaphors risking unintelligibility, or totally lacking; ensuing behavior can oscillate between quietism and hyper-activity. Collected together, these appearances form a fairly regular syndrome, altogether analogous to a seizure; to the behaviorist, it can only be regarded as an essential psychological disorder. Further, since similar disorders can be observed as a consequence of either abnormal physiological processes or drugs, there would seem to be little of philosophical interest in such phenomena; perhaps a cure is suggested.

On the other hand, nothing of what the external observer observes constitutes the sense of the experience for the mystic himself. When he recovers his wits, he will tell us in some fashion or other that he has experienced his identity with God, the *absolute*, or *nothingness*. None of the objectively observable symptoms form any part of his account. On the contrary, with his language varying according to the philosophical or religious rhetoric of his preference, the experience was of *reality*, was the perfection of knowledge, and can even serve as an absolute ground for ethics or a holiness beyond good and evil.

Philosophy, which keeps watch over such extraordinary claims and counter-claims, surely has here a problem which it must resolve. Its obligation to do so does not arise, of course, from any interest in solving miscellaneous problems at random; it does arise from the seriousness of the mystic's claims, which manage sooner or later to touch upon virtually every legitimate interest of man. To form a fair estimate of these extraordinary claims, it is axiomatic to adopt a point of view from which the sense of the claims of both sides to the dispute can appear. In a word, honesty forbids us from choosing a method or perspective from whose point of view one or the other side vanishes into absurdity or invisibility. Our method, then, cannot be one which guarantees a specific answer to our question; that answer can only emerge from the concrete investigation. These considerations recommend phenomenology as the appropriate method; it aims at being without presuppositions, and has a peculiar aptitude both for investigating the structures of inner life as they are to the mind living them, and to assess the claims of external observation. But what is "phenomenology," in what sense will we use it, and what is its priority?

A. The Primacy of Phenomenology

1. Phenomenology, as here understood, is an open reflection upon consciousness and what consciousness is conscious of, the *ego-cogito-cogitatum*. It is therefore a point of view or an intellectual posture of the spirit, an intuitive reflection. It has, as its subject matter, the phenomenal, that is, that which shows itself as it shows itself, without the distortion or prejudice of extraneous beliefs, postulates, or logical principles. It is not primarily a deductive procedure, although, of course, there could be a phenomenology of deduction, too. To reflection, that which shows itself with immediacy is not simply objectivities in their "world," but also, and correlatively, my consciousness of those things. Hence, the phenomenon for reflection is my consciousness of the objective, a totality, in which consciousness is related to the objective through "intentionality." My perceptual consciousness — or perception, in short — aims at, means, or intends its own unique domain of perceptual objects, which are taken in an ensemble as the world, insofar as it is accessible to perception. But my consciousness is hardly exhausted by perception, nor is the world merely a world of perceptual objects. Indeed, even for common sense, the world is inexhaustible in the depths of its structures, and so is my consciousness of it. For not merely do we perceive, but we remember, imagine, dream, love, hate, will, as well as think abstractly. Each mode of consciousness addresses itself to its own appropriate domain of objectivity, intends it, and implicates itself with that domain according to principle. Further, various modes of consciousness are interrelated, as are various structures of the world; these subjective–objective interrelations are themselves matters of phenomenological dependence; for example, could we remember, if we had never perceived, or — correlatively and objectively — could there be a past which was never present?

If the proper subject matter of phenomenology is the phenomenon, and if the phenomenon itself has both a subjective and an objective pole, then that point of view from which this whole phenomenological field is visible is radical reflection, the ego bending back upon itself but already provided with an objective field; that ego is the reflexive subject of itself and the world.

If some such thing is a general description of the "phenomenon," the whole project might look like some introspective psychology. Husserl himself never tired of distinguishing phenomenology from psychology, and the distinction is radical. Introspective psychology, in which I reflect upon my experiences and derive from that reflection certain empirical laws supposedly valid for the most part for all or most, does not even envisage what the phenomenologist looks for. The phenomenologist, through the so-called eidetic reduction, looks for the essence or structure exhibited by the facts of psychic life. Those factual occurrences in my psyche, in all their qualitative differences, do indeed exhibit structures or essences, or they would be nothing whatsoever. And each psychic event, taken as a moment in my factual psychic life, no doubt exhibits a great number of essences; in fact, as Plato proves, these concrete, factual events are but muddy images of the knowledge of *form*. No matter; once they have offered up some essence to reflection, the reflecting phenomenologist forgets them as facts and has no further use for them; he is not in the least interested in factual descriptions of events which, by that time, have already vanished, but rather in articulations of the essence they have — or perhaps have not — exemplified. The service of the fact is over, and we have something better, the essence it seemed to embody for a moment. Phenomenology, then, is or seeks to be a cognition of essential connections, and of course not any essential connections seized at random, but those fundamental essential connections between consciousness and its determinate world which are foundational. The interest in essential connections is expressed in the "-logy" of phenomenology. The essence disentangled from fact was at first seen in the facts of psychic life; it was or seemed to be embodied there, a "concrete" logic, not in the least formal. But whether any given moment of my psychic life was actually an instance of that essence or of another is of no interest to the phenomenologist. Thus, the essential structure of perception is what it is, whether any given instance of my consciousness was an act of perception in any pure sense or not.

With this brief sketch of what we shall adopt in Husserl's phenomenology for our present purposes, a number of questions immediately arise: if phenomenology is a personal and radical reflection upon the direct life of consciousness in order to grasp its essential sense, what chance does the mystic have, in his convulsions and ecstasies, of reflecting upon his own conscious experience — an experience, moreover, whose very sense is to deny the finality of all distinctions, that between himself the subject, his "object" God, as well as that between the mystic experience itself and reflection? In a word, is not the phenomenology of mystic experience doomed from the start, by virtue of its intellectual or reflective character? Further, is there not either an absurdity or at least a fantastic optimism involved in the effort to make God, being, or the absolute *phenomenal*? The Greeks said: "He who sees God must die." But questions such as these cannot be answered at once; they shall have to be answered sooner or later, but since they conceal within themselves certain presuppositions as to what is possible, what is sayable, what is true, we shall for the moment suspend them, and return to them after more concrete approaches.

In any event, our aim is to elicit by reflection upon mystic experience its own inherent sense to the mystic, its very essence as embodied in mystic consciousness. That sense will be questioned, since only it is at stake. And if at the beginning the phenomenological evidence shall be drawn from the vast literature on the subject and therefore might seem to rest upon second-hand and therefore questionable reports, at the end we hope to make it evident that the mystic essence in question, while spectacularly evident in convulsive mystics, is at the same time pervasive of common experience. It is so pervasive, in fact, that no human experience is at all possible without the implicit governing of that structure. At least the pervasiveness of the essential structure was also a conclusion which William James reached, along other routes. The truth is that, far from being inarticulate or lost in the ineffable, the mystics are almost too articulate, can hardly stop talking. In fact, their best texts are so expressive that readers hostile or not otherwise known for their sympathy to mysticism find themselves secretly understanding the whole business. Would that be possible if mysticism were confined to the abrupt or convulsive experiences undergone, after all, by only a few?

2. *The ontological question*, namely, whether there is, in fact, any external reality corresponding to what the mystic affirms or, on the contrary, whether the whole affair is not rather a fiction of a disturbed brain — this question is clearly secondary to the phenomenological explication of what it is the mystic is affirming. What could be more obvious than the principle that the very question whether something exists or not is senseless until we have clarified what it is whose existence is being affirmed or denied? Further, as we shall have occasion to develop later, essentially different types of things have essentially different modes of being. "Existence" itself is but one such mode appropriate for certain kinds of things and essentially inappropriate for others. Hence if there "are" platonic forms, they could not possibly exist in any sense univocal with the existence of historical events or sensible entities. In a word, being, or how something is, must be modulated following the kind of thing to which being is attributed. Ontological questions, then, must be strictly attentive to what sort of thing is said to be, and to the mode of being which it could possibly have. These discriminations do not prejudge any issue; they only make the issues statable.

3. *Epistemological questions*, which ask whether mystic experience is cognitive of anything, similarly, are strictly posterior to the phenomenological explication of that experience itself. Knowledge with its correlate, the "cognitive," must it-

self be modulated along with the modes of being; we must discriminate modes of knowing.

Without such distinctions, nothing could be less surprising than a degradation of the claims of mystic experience — through a simple analysis of it — to feelings, sense perception or scientific hypothesis. If these modes of knowledge rest inherently upon an agreement or adjustment of judgment to an external object, it is obvious that mystic experience claiming an immediate awareness of an absolute neither external nor internal to it must fail to pass muster. But then it is exactly the mystic's experience which can challenge the model of cognition of an external world. Further, whether mystic experience is or is not cognitive of any reality whatsoever depends on the preceding question, whether its "reality" is a reality and in what sense.

4. *Priority of phenomenology.* For some, all these questions are extinguished by causal considerations. If the phenomenological, ontological, and epistemological questions seem to carry us beyond anything scientifically ascertainable, with causes we seem to be on firm ground. The modifications of chromosomes, connections between neurones, in short, psychochemistry, will "one day" explain the phenomenon, and will answer the questions posed above. But here we are at the farthest remove from any fundamental inquiry. The truth is that, from the causal point of view, nothing whatsoever can be asked pertinent to the questions mentioned above; the very sense of the questions vanishes.

For the moment, one could easily grant that every time a drug was injected, a mystic vision occurred. Precisely what would such a circumstance contribute to the questions above, whether that experience was a cognitive apprehension of the identity of the subject and the absolute? What is mystic experience for some abrupt or convulsive mystics has behavioral analogies with experiences conditioned by or with antecedents in epileptic discharges, sexual hysteria, glandular disturbances or the ingestion of drugs; one can easily grant that the heterogeneity of mystic experience measured against daily life requires some such radical disturbance of the organism to be released. But it does not in any way follow either that the experience itself was produced by such conditions, or that the possible sense or validity of the experience is in any way discussable in these terms. No doubt, if mystic experience occurs, all the conditions for its occurrence must obtain. But this empty tautology, which is equally valid and equally empty for ordinary experience itself, is in principle incapable of addressing itself to the sense of phenomenological, ontological or epistemological questions. Even for common mathematics, if I judge one to equal one, the meaning of that judgment and its validity are not statable in terms of events of a psychic order, linked to their psychic or physical antecedents. No doubt it is true that I could not make the actual judgment if I were not alive, my heart beating, my brain fed with oxygen; but what could be more evident than that the sense and truth of the judgment is not ascertainable or even available to any study of my brain, heart or body; nor of antecedent psychic events, taken in their factual character rather than their logical implication. It is the logical dimension which wholly disappears from any empirical inquiry into causes; and yet it is the logical character of these experiences which we address ourselves to in pheneno*logy*.

Finally, the entirety of causal investigations into mystic experience presupposes the phenomenological. The so-called causes must be causes of what? Precisely the phenomenon as it is to him who experiences it, and not something else altogether. But the phenomenon as it is to the subject, in its logical essence, is what phenomenology is designed to explicate. Hence, the inevitable gap in physiological explanations; they explain, even at best, only physiological events, metabolism, swooning, etc.; but, as we noted above, these phenomena form no part of the mystic's own account of how it was for him, and frequently he has to be informed by spectators what all these symptoms were. The gap is between the externally observable symptoms and the inner sense of the phenomenon. Further, if the mystic's claim of the validity of his experience holds up, and if his experience cannot be truly characterized *without the actual presence of the absolute*, it will be clear, without further ado, that *no* physiological account could possibly be adequate unless the absolute itself be classified among the "physiological" causes. Causes must be adequate to their effects.

B. Dialectical Phenomenology

The phenomenological field opened up to radical reflection is primary, supplying both the source of the problem and the only possible source of the solution, but what more precisely is it? Initially, it is simply I myself aware of what is not myself, a field of objects. And since I cannot be aware of what I cannot be aware of, nor can I be aware of something without having something to be aware of, it appears intuitively obvious to phenomenological reflection that there is a strict and necessary correlation between the phenomenological object and the phenomenological subject. Stated thus formally, it looks like a verbal truism. And it is indeed a tautology, but one with infinite consequences, as we shall see. In any case, it is hardly dubitable.

Phenomenology was frequently described as "eidetic-descriptive" by Husserl himself; eidetic, since it aims at intuitions of essence rather than contingent fact, descriptive, since it wishes to be intuitively passive *vis-à-vis* its subjective–objective field, presupposing nothing, and not primarily either deductive or inductive. It simply wants to see what the world is like as it must look to me or any other, and to characterize that phenomenon in terms most appropriate to each unique type of mind-object correlation. And while this characterization of phenomenology could hardly be questioned, perhaps it could also be misleading. It was originally chosen to distinguish the phenomenological attitude from what it was *not*, an empirical psychological science on the one hand, or an idealistic rational construction of what the world must be, on the other. The formula would be misleading, however, if it concealed the actual phenomenological task posed by the aim of phenomenology itself. In a word, neither the intuition nor the description in question could imply that phenomenological analysis consisted of intuitively staring at something already completely disclosed at a glance, in order to give out descriptions of the obvious. Husserl himself had utter contempt for this "picture-book" phenomenology.

The intuition was always a final, hoped-for accomplishment; never an assured beginning. Ideally, it is always possible; but in fact, it is more a flickering and fragile outcome of phenomenological work. Intuition, then, with its accompanying importance as the only source of true evidence and its correlative ideal, certainly is, in fact, an intermittent and always questionable psychological event. Husserl's insistence upon its fundamental character was itself a claim only for the essence of intuition, and not a claim about any particular event in anyone's mind. That Husserl made intuition the very ground of phenomenology was, of course, absolutely consistent with his exclusive interest in rigorous and essential connections, always matters of principle and not of fact. For a man to claim that he personally lived in the domain of certain and immediate vision, thereby in one stroke confusing essence and fact, would be at the same time a radical phenomenological error and an intolerable case of arrogance.

"Description" has also some misleading suggestions. Little could be more tedious than reading descriptions of things — travel literature about the country in which one has always lived. Everything, then, depends upon precisely what one understands by "description." In Husserl's later work, and even as early as the *Ideas I. II. III.* phenomenological description was understood as "intentional analysis." They are, of course, the same, but then the emphasis is different; to signal the difference, we shall use here a term which Husserl would have rejected, "dialectical" phenomenology, Husserl rejecting it for its "Hegelian" connotations, and we ourselves using it for its emphasis upon the *implications* of objects. At any rate, whether "intentional" or "dialectical," the description aimed at by phenomenology is never the product of simply staring at a variety of things and trying to put into words what is seen. It is an effort to render explicit the meanings of things as they are given; and things do not simply mean themselves. Their very essence as meant by us is to indicate other things; they themselves implicitly "intend" or "signify" other things, and the explicit excavation of those intentions is their intentional analysis.

But, following our tautology above, establishing the strict correlation between the subjective and the objective, the objective meanings of things themselves are also at the same time our own meanings, insofar as we follow the things themselves. Plato has Socrates demand of us that we "follow the argument *(logos)*." If we do follow the *logos*, or if we do indeed, with Husserl, revert "back to the things themselves," then insofar as we do, our subjective intentions are in accord with those objectified meanings which things are. The subjective and objective will be in accord, although still distinguishable. The essential ideal accord will be to that extent realized in fact; and since it is a realization, we can easily say that the strict and necessary correlation between the subjective and objective so realized is an accomplishment *(Leistung)* of the transcendental ego.

That this accomplishment, realized in intuition, need not occur in us is more obvious than that it ideally could. What is more obvious than our losing track of our own intentions, our more frequently imposing extraneous, arbitrary, imagined, customary associations upon the very given itself, rather than following our own intentions directly to the object? Or what more obvious than our talking without following the argument? In fact, this is the more customary meaning of subjective, to wit, that it is the whimsical, private, erratic, or personal side of us which menaces knowledge with opinion, and is to be eschewed at all costs. But yet its opposite, objective knowledge, is also subjective, or else no one could have it or even dream of it. Intentional or dialectical analysis, then, is not in the least tracing *my* own meanings and intentions as they wander here and there, but tracing those intentions only insofar as they are in strict correlation with the objective significations of the given object. Otherwise, I have not analyzed the object but only myself, and myself only in my factual, existential, and accidental states.

If Husserl himself had little taste for Hegelian or any other dialectics, it was no doubt because he regarded it as intellectual construction, making things go where opinion thought they *ought* rather than the fresh and presuppositionless following of what was given in its own bodily presence with its own characteristic categories and style. On the other hand, and for all their differences, both Hegel and Husserl, precisely through following the objective logic of the phenomena themselves, became caught up in teleology; Hegel explicitly, and Husserl only late and implicitly, where again and again the source of all world meanings was found in that "wonder of all wonders," the ego—and, if the source of all meanings, then the ultimate solution to the enigma of the world. Intentional or dialectical analysis went *somewhere*; the world of objectivities was not simply a heap of things and properties accidentally displaying itself before me and which could be any which way in every respect. The worldliness of the world, or what it is to be a world—while in its first appearances seemingly a found datum and indeed constituting the very essence of the objective—is in point of fact both found and also transcendentally constituted by my own transcendental ego as well as that of every other. It is a meaning conferred, part of that meaning being "that which I must always find external to myself." If I had not spontaneously and also necessarily constituted such a meaning, then that objective meaning in and of itself would be meaningless to me, not even retaining the sense objective or independent of my own particular subjectivity. If in thought I suppress all thought of subjectivity, clearly even independence of subjectivity instantly loses its sense. Nor can I be surprised by novelties, the unexpected, the undiscovered, disconfirmations of my expectations, and whatever else characterizes the existential-empirical, if there is no I in any sense to be surprised. Husserl's phenomenology, then, particularly in its late phases, took a deep interest in these ultimate questions, the final but perhaps never-to-be-completed inter-structuring of objective and subjective essences. These find their solution not in miscellanies of descriptions, but in an ultimate teleology in the whole phenomenological field of subject-object; and their essential unity of meaning is always traced back to that "wonder of all wonders," the transcendental ego.

And, of course, for Hegel too the ultimate embodied logic of the spirit is finally to recover itself after its objective expressions, precisely in those various objectifications in nature and in its own historical acts: a recovery of itself in an absolute knowledge which does not obliterate distinctions but preserves them and interrelates them in a teleology which accomplishes itself in absolute knowledge.

These are not altogether tangential questions to our own inquiry into mysticism, and yet they carry us into the historical, into interpretations of interpretations. But, aside from that, it is clear that both the phenomenology of Hegel and that of Husserl were open to a phenomenology of mysticism, even when such was never planned by Husserl and no doubt would have been loathed by the old logician. The matter is only mentioned because my own purport is to develop as rigorously as possible an intentional or dialectical analysis of the mystic experience. This analysis will be dialectical in two senses: first, the phenomenon must be raised from a vague, hidden, implicit phenomenon to some degree of explicit phenomenality. Second, the factors within mystic experience, always myself and the absolute, must be dialectically perceived to be identical or essentially united in and of their own essence. Both of these tasks demand discursive analysis; the analytic discussion of any experience, mystic or not, is obviously not that experience itself nor a substitute for it. Nor is the experience its own analysis.

Dialectic is "talking through," or, in a word, bringing out what is hidden. What results at the end is and is not the same as what we began with; it is the same subject matter, but what was hidden or confused at the beginning is now a bit clearer. As clearer, it is different; as the clarification of something it is the same. No doubt, at the end, everything will be ineffable; but even that can be approached by what is effable and discursive, and its ineffability will itself be clarified. Our own dialectic will show that even such opposition as the ineffable and the effable are themselves finally reversible such that the ineffable, unspeakable, unthinkable itself is the sole intelligibility, and contrariwise what had up to that time seemed clear and reasonable enough is, mystically considered, absolutely unintelligible in itself. However this is all by way of anticipation.

C. Imaginative Variations

If our intention is to elicit the universal essence of the mystic experience and make it evident to intuition so that its claims may be evaluated, we must display clear examples of its expression. Fortunately, world literature provides us with more than enough of these examples, drawn, moreover, from the most diverse cultures. We shall look into these expressions in order to see wherein the invariant, universal essence lies, and what in them is accidental and therefore dispensable for our purposes, even though not necessarily for the mystic's own.

The variation of example might just as well be conducted in the imagination; but for the purposes of stabilizing the discussion, we shall, for the most part, limit ourselves to historical examples. It is obvious that some examples approach and others recede from some polar type; it is that type we are looking for. Now, the polar type is itself determined by a "pretheoretical" sense of what is and what is not "mystical." It might seem that the pre-theoretical sense of what we are looking for turns the whole enterprise into something hopelessly arbitrary and whimsical; might not another have different pre-theoretical sense of an essence he could with "equal right" call "mystical"? Now then, our questioner might ask, who is right? In the long run, is not each simply defining a *word*, and would not a good dictionary of usage resolve the entire problem?

But it is not in the least our purpose to arbitrate meanings of a word. It is to elicit *one* essence and examine it; if others see other essences covered by the same term, find and good; let them analyze those others. In any event, the analysis is aimed at an essence, and what that essence dictates, and not into a word and what its historical usages might dictate.

That these are two enterprises is obvious. An essence is a structure all of whose factors or discriminable parts are bound together by the same necessity which binds together the center and circumference of a circle. It is therefore a whole of parts whose parts are unthinkable in isolation. In fact, they are hardly mechanical parts at all, but more closely, organic factors, or more closely yet, logical factors. On the other hand, the various meanings which a single word might bear have no such logical or organic interconnection, but are united through historical accidents of usage or sometimes, as Wittgenstein says, through "family resemblances." It is clear, then, that the principles unifying the discussion in the two cases are radically different. But this, of course, need not prevent us from picking up clues from language, insofar as they are clues for our own purposes and controlled by our own criteria.

We shall then be looking for something, and we shall call it mystical; if someone else wants to call it something else, or finds something lacking which would be appropriate to another pre-theoretical sense, there can be no quarrel.

In all this, the clearest examples will serve our purposes best; our use of examples is only to make something clear, and vague, mixed, or remote examples could only muddy the waters. But then what is clear and what unclear? Spinoza said that an adequate or true idea is the measure of both itself as adequate and of the false, and we shall follow. The best, that is, clearest examples therefore will have a normative role against which mixed examples and illustrations will be measured. We are not then looking for some lowest common denominator of all possible instances, but a range of clear instances of something we call the mystic, in order to make intuitively evident an invariant essence, which will serve as our subject matter.

Chapter II **Absolute Reality**

The mystic expresses the union of his soul with God. Or is it only the belief or the delusion of that union? What if there is no God, nor soul, let alone their union? And above all, what is a "union"? And if there were such a union, could it be known to be such by that soul; and if so, what are the consequences?

All these questions shall be looked into in due time; meanwhile we must make what will certainly seem like a willful and perverse move: the term "God" will be replaced by "absolute reality." The reason for this neutralization is largely clarity of discussion in an area notorious for its ambiguity. The term "God," naming as it does the most ancient interest of mankind, could hardly fail to accumulate around itself the entire history of the thought and passion of men. Any term so freighted is entirely unsuitable for our purposes; on the other hand, "absolute reality" is so abstract, quaint, out-of-fashion, and almost meaningless that it will serve our purposes admirably. We shall investigate it; if some find it to some extent coinciding with their personal God, fine and good, if not, not; it will have its own logic. By this means perhaps we can disintoxicate the discussion from 2,000 years of enthusiasms for or against God, along with questions hinging upon religion, church, myth, ritual, and creed. No doubt, the choice of "absolute reality" will offend some mystics themselves, announcing from the beginning that this is to be a rational investigation; and who indeed are more famous for their irrationalism than the mystics? Nevertheless, while the mystics may be right in denouncing a certain form of rationalism, they may be in serious error in imagining that what they hate in reason exhausts reason itself, or is anything but a very limited form of it.

Since the term "reality" will be figuring prominently in the succeeding discussion, it might be well to examine its meaning with some care. This meaning will be its meaning in this discussion, and not necessarily elsewhere. Our aim, as mentioned above, is phenomenological and not philological; we would like to trace essential implications of an essence and not the history of words. This is particularly important now, since as anyone can verify for himself the term "reality," let alone "absolute," has fallen almost completely out of philosophical usage. The disappearance of a meaning from a language has serious consequences when it affects thought as well; what once could be said is now senseless, and continuity with human thought is disrupted; but sooner or later that suppressed meaning reappears in some unrecognizable form, along with the attendant naïveté of a supposed discovery. And yet that whole process is not entirely useless; meanings become stale with repetition, words are repeated without a re-enactment of their sense, and the deterioration of mind requires rejuvenation.

Philosophy and hence phenomenology pursue the truth of reality, reality and truth being correlates. Reality, then, is what truly is. Consequently, the term "reality" has its own function in any thought which is philosophical. That the term "reality," like the term "God," has had so many meanings is but testimony to the variety of possible true philosophies. Again, we choose it here precisely because of its *dead* character; as an empty vessel we can fill it with almost whatever fluids we please without violating usage. Besides, it is a term some mystics are most friendly with and, not by accident, also has a long philosophical tradition.

But at the moment nothing seems more metaphysical — or, for some, senseless — than a discussion of reality. The *ontological argument* for the existence of God which we shall look into in a moment and which has a very close connection with mystic experience, rests entirely upon notions like "higher" or "lower" degrees of reality, "a most perfect being," "that than which there can be no greater," etc., depending upon the formulation. But these degrees of *being* or reality are wholly senseless in a framework of thought in which things either are or are not, exist or do not exist. Consequently, in the reduction of reality to existence, the very sense of the ontological argument is lost and, with that loss, any attempt to prove or refute it on formal logical grounds is itself misguided; the refutations or proofs rest upon mistaken formulations, formulations of what was never intended. If things either are or are not, then indeed what does it mean to attribute to their existence a higher or lower degree? And so, evidently, the higher and lower degrees of reality are very improperly translated into "is" or "is not"; fact or non-fact; existence or nonexistence. Something else was intended, without the firm grasp of which the ontological argument is wholly unintelligible. Unintelligibility, however, is not a refutation, but simply the disappearance of a meaning from view. An essential step, then, is a recovery of the sense of the ontological argument. That it is no discursive argument at all but, in fact, one aspect of the essence of the mystic experience, an articulation of a rational intuition of absolute reality, will be our first contention. Other ways, each of which has its appropriate articulation, will then be discussed.

A. The Ontological Argument

From Anselm through Descartes and Spinoza, and on through the moderns, the *ontological argument* for the existence — or better, the reality — of God has assumed two forms. In one, we begin with the idea of an infinitely perfect being; but if the idea of the infinitely perfect being were *only* an idea, then indeed it would not be infinitely perfect, but would lack objective existence. Hence that being of which we have an idea must also exist. In another version, we begin with the essence of an infinitely perfect being; but if the infinitely perfect being were merely an essence, that is, a bare possibility, it would lack a perfection, to wit actual existence; hence it must necessarily exist. Or, put otherwise, its existence follows from its essence. In effect, the arguments are one: an infinitely perfect essence or nature cannot be merely as the fictive object of thought, as a bare possibility which would require additional evidence, external to its own given nature, to assure thought of its existence "outside" thought. Or, abstracting from the question whether it is thought or not, its essence by its own essential character is impossible without that essence also being. The argument could easily be recast in terms of language. We define a perfect being; but then that perfect being must also exist independently of our definitions, or it is not that defined being. And so, three times over, there is an infinitely perfect reality, it must necessarily exist, and it is, formally considered, identical with that of which we have formed an idea or definition. We add "identical" since if the perfect being which formed the object of our idea were different from the really existing perfect being, such that the object or our idea only represented the perfect being itself, we would in effect have two perfect beings, or again our idea of the real perfect being would be false. Consequently, the perfect being which forms the object of our idea is one and the same as the perfect being itself. In effect, therefore, there is one place where thought is not busying itself with representations or symbols of something lying beyond it, but with the reality itself. Its object and the reality are one and the same. The idea of a perfect being, consequently, is an intuition of a reality and not a representative concept of something else, or of something which has only a putative existence. In a word, at this point, reason which "forms" such an idea is intuitive and envisages rationally perfect being in itself.

And here two side notes might be observed: any rational system of philosophy must at some point anchor the truths of reason in reality, or the entire system floats away into a sheer possibility-hypothesis or fictional construction. It is hardly by accident, then, that both Descartes and Spinoza insisted upon the validity of the argument. But in effect, the ontological argument is hardly an "argument" either, at least not an argument in discursive or inferential form. In any version, the argument, to whatever extent it is an argument, merely denies an absurdity: that my idea of an infinite being is not true of that being, that is, is indeed not an idea of it, but of something else. The argument exposes the absurdity of supposing it is of something else. In its second version, the essence of an infinite being of its own essential nature necessarily involves the being of that essence; the argument rejects the reduction of that being to an additional accident to be added to the essence synthetically. Therefore, both versions rest upon either an idea or an essence of the perfect being and simply deny that that essence or idea can be other than it is. In modern terms, therefore, they simply affirm what we now call a phenomenological or eidetic truth: reason formally intuits perfect being, and this intuition of its own nature neither requires nor can tolerate any further evidence to guarantee its own intuitive content. "Back to the things themselves" was Husserl's slogan; and here indeed we have a "thing itself" to which we have reverted, and moreover a thing of most extraordinary consequences. The *lumen naturale* of Descartes, or the *adequate idea* of Spinoza now have as their intentional aim an infinitely perfect reality, given intuitively, and in self-evidence.

Secondly, such an idea, by its own essence, could hardly be formed, generated, or invented by us; out of what could it be made? It is hardly the composition of anything, nor is it an abstraction from imperfect realities which are clearly unsuitable for the job. If it is not inferred from what is less perfect than itself, nor put together by some synthetic power of the imagination or reason, let alone the power of speech, it is, precisely as all thinkers of this being have insisted, innate to rational consciousness. To say that the idea of perfect being is innate does not imply, of course, that anyone's waking and explicit attention is permanently devoted to that being. Obviously, in that respect, the idea may remain latent to waking attention throughout the life of the mind. But this question touches only the particular mode of awareness which the mind has of that extraordinary infinite idea innate to it, and as we shall argue further on, not innate to it as one idea among many, but as constitutive of reason's very essence. The essence of reason essentially implicates perfect being as its intentional object. The essentiality of this relation makes rational intuition possible.

B. The Notion of Absolute Reality

The above analyses of the ontological argument must seem hopelessly abstract to carry the weight claimed for that argument and, no doubt, as perhaps the least convincing approach to mystic experience itself. One difficulty lies in giving sense to anything as abstract as infinite or absolute reality.

But if we assume the phenomenological position and reflect first upon common experience as it occurs in each person, nothing could be less contestable than that our continuing experience is an experience always of somethings-or-other. We could say "things" simply, if that term were not to be understood as restricting the experience to substances, or even identities of any sort. Our "somethings-or-other" should be understood, then, as the name for any object of experience or of any object of any mode of consciousness whatsoever. Such objects, things, or somethings would consequently comprise things in the ordinary sense, but also their qualities, quantities, positions, movements, interactions, generations, and destructions, as well as abstract objects, such as numbers, principles, laws, values, or the objects of ideas of whatever sort. There could be no possibility of an exhaustive enumeration of what could possibly be an object of consciousness, nor is there any need for it. The domain of objectivity, so understood, is indefinite. We are in effect talking about the world and the infinite number of ways in which the world can present itself to us, be divided, classified, idealized, conceptualized; it presents itself to us as an infinitely explorable domain, a domain infinitely variously conceivable, and infinitely problematic.

And if this domain seems large enough, it must be enlarged even further. For consciousness is hardly limited to cognitive experience, looking, seeing, or talking about. It also dreams, remembers, imagines. It loves, hates, is indifferent to, fears, prizes; further, it wills, decides, and acts. Each of these modes of consciousness — and our list here is not and could never be exhaustive — has its appropriate intention and intentional object, though its intentional object would hardly be an object for sight or cognitive experience. And yet, each of these distinctive modes of consciousness, in its unique way, discloses another domain of reality, or another face of it, and in every case the intentional object is distinguishable in essence from the subjective act intending it — distinguishable yet in necessary correlation.

Out of such continuing living experience, we provisionally isolate this or that for attention; this or that, be it what it may, is now an explicit object, nameable, discussable, analyzable. The isolation of this or that object can be a function, of course, of an arbitrary act of attention; or, on the other hand, it can isolate itself for attention — by moving, by having brilliant colors, or by standing out through its remarkable properties. Even arbitrary directions of attention would be impossible unless that which we attended to had some differential character to which we could direct our attention. But obviously, for the most part, what occupies our attention is an object which interests us, that most primitively menaces or attracts us in our living existence, which is not in the least to deny a supervening curiosity little related to living experience. In any event, we are not concerned with the psychology of attention, but only to remark that each of these objects, no matter what they may be, and no matter how they have forced themselves upon our attention, is indeed a something-or-other, is what it is, has a character or essence, forms the content of experience, and is therefore reality. About any such reality we can ask what it is, whether it exists or not, if it exists, whether it exists as we think it does, etc. But without the domain of objectivity or objective realities, we would obviously have nothing whatsoever before our experience, or nothing whatsoever to experience.*

If any particular object or reality presents itself to us as a something-or-other, at the same stroke it presents itself as a something which cannot be what it is except in relation to other somethings-or-other. In a word, each particular object

*Cf. the author's *Objectivity: An Essay in Phenomenological Ontology* (New York: Times Books, 1968).

declares of itself that it is a *relative* reality; it is then an eidetic truth that no particular thing can be what it is in essential disconnection from other things. Consequently each relative reality, or particular object, declares of its own essence that there is an absolute reality, which in and of itself is not a particular object essentially contingent upon others.

The *experience* of the provisional, relative, and insubstantial character of things in the world is, of course, the beginning of mystic experience — which aims finally at a reversal of that experience into an experience of absolute reality itself no longer relative to, nor a part or phase or mode of anything else. The intellectual demonstration of the essential insufficiency of any finite object or collection of them is the heart of philosophical metaphysics when it takes itself seriously. But then, the "experience" in mystical experience is not itself precisely ordinary experience bound, as it usually is, to the practical. It is already an experience which asks a philosophical question; by going to the essential heart of what is experienced, it experiences the essential insufficiency of each thing. But neither is the metaphysical intuition of the insufficiency of each finite thing an affair of abstract reasoning or inference. Reasoning or inference could only carry the mind from one thing to another equally finite thing; the insufficiency of the entire process could only be thought by a thought of that absolute *not* met with in any stage of the process. And what thought indeed is it, but that of the *perfect reality* envisaged in the ontological argument? If then at first sight we contrast mystic experience with metaphysical intuition, only the slightest reflection is enough to see that, in essence, they are one and the same. In essence only, since in fact mystic experience can immediately acquire the barnacles of imagination and desire and deteriorate into rank superstition, while metaphysical thought quickly degenerates into abstraction and empty language. But the essence is identical, for in the genuine core, obviously, absolute reality is not a fit object for the imagination, nor could its idea possibly be an abstraction. It must be the most concrete of all.

The arguments above are, with intention, very general. "Insufficiency," "relational," "insubstantial," etc. characterize the finite in most universal terms. This is necessary for our present purposes in order to avoid staking our argument on some particular world-scheme or system of the world. To determine specifically how any particular thing is dependent upon other particular things would rest upon a scientific or other hypothesis concerning what the particular thing really was. But our own argument hardly depends upon any such hypothesis; no matter what the particular thing is, in its particularity it must essentially depend upon other things that are not itself.

Further, the modes of dependence would vary as we pass from type to type of thing. If physical events depend *causally* upon other physical events, one region of space is not causally related to its surroundings, nor one period of time to another. Nor are human beings causally dependent upon their environment in the same way. Nor are numbers dependent upon one another in any way univocal with spatial, temporal, causal or voluntary relations. Again, the modes of dependence are indefinitely various, each appropriate for its own range of objects. Correspondingly, the ways in which modes of extension in Spinoza's system depend upon one another, extensionally, differ from the ways in which modes under the attribute of thought depend upon one another. For Hegel, although the stages of *absolute mind* are all dialectically related, the literal sense of "dialectic" varies with each stage. We should like our own argument to be as general as possible, independent of any specific world formula, and for that reason use logical terms of the utmost generality. The specification of these general terms would give a good deal more life to the argument, but would deprive it of the required generality.

As for absolute reality, it will be that which is not dependent upon any other thing or reality, hence ontologically perfect. As such, it cannot, of its own essence, be a member of any series of relative or finite realities. It may of course — and indeed must — be itself related to these finite things, but that mode of relation is not univocal with the relations of dependence those things have among one another. The usual ways of describing this unique relation eternally subsisting between absolute reality and finite things is creation, or effulgence, emanation, even degradation, falling, dissipation, etc. Or things are seen as specializations, particularizations, developments, modes, parts, illusions, veils, etc. of absolute reality. In any case, however, the particular things are not related to absolute reality as things outside that reality but as parts or phases of it. Hence the principle is preserved that absolute reality is not dependent upon what is other to itself, but only to itself, now taken particularly, serially or relatively. The world taken altogether throughout its physical and its temporal extent is finally one and not many, and proceeds in its particularization and serialization from what is itself absolutely one, that is, absolute reality.

Various finite things realize in their reality closer and more and more approximate analogies to absolute reality; material substances more than the indeterminate spatio-temporal medium out of which they individuate themselves, living things more than material things, and mind more than mere organic life. If absolute reality is ontologically perfect, these imperfect realities nevertheless qualitatively approach the understood perfection of absolute reality; they are therefore of themselves ranked in hierarchies, or degrees, of perfection.

Our essential point here is that reality admits of degree and hierarchy, whereas existence does not; existence, with its either/or character, is, so to speak, the lowest common denominator of real things, wholly abstracting precisely from their reality. In their reality, their natures or essences are necessarily in a hierarchy of perfection, both reflecting and dependent upon absolute reality. It is no surprise, then, that a purely formal logic can have nothing to do with that reality from which it has withdrawn in its formalization, and can only employ modal operators which derive from bare existence: existence, possible existence, necessary existence. We should say that all this is not so much false as intentionally empty. It does become false when it extends its claims beyond their proper domain and denies the sense or validity of mystical or metaphysical intuitions, which are, on the face of them, intuitions into reality. That, in the course of arguments over the ontological argument, the term "existence" is used by both sides, as in the existence or non-existence of God, only bears witness to an amphiboly in linguistic usage: if the partisans of the ontological argument have assumed that existence applied to God was univocal with the same word applied to islands, the enemies of the argument have a point. The term is not univocally applicable to perfect and imperfect realities. Which is not to deny existence to absolute reality but, as Hegel said, merely to attribute to the most perfect of all, the most poverty-stricken category of all, bare existence; but the enemies of the argument, the formal logicians, have equally overlooked the mode of being truly applicable to absolute reality: eternal being. As the origin of mere existence, absolute reality is not an existent thing nor a member of the series of existent things, but rather their absolute ontological perfection. God is certainly not an existent if He is conceived as the origin of existence. As Plato demonstrated, the eternal forms of being are not themselves events or things in becoming or generation. Their being is identical with their essence, and is the kind of being which can only pertain to essence. Plotinus dwells on the fact that *the One* is beyond being.

In a word, absolute reality is that essence which is not dependent in any fashion whatsoever upon any other essence or thing, and which *is* in the only essentially appropriate fashion for it to be; it eternally is. Bare existence is that mode of being appropriate to relative or finite things in their relativity, and is a synonym for Plato's genesis or becoming, which he characterizes as a "moving image of eternity."

C. Degrees of Perfection

"Perfection" is not exactly a term in common contemporary metaphysical usage. It derives, of course, from the meaning of having been "made through to the end", "finished," "accomplished." Its primordial sense here is taken to be *ontological* and not initially moral or aesthetic, which would present derived meanings. If we were to approach the meaning of perfection — with its attendant senses of hierarchy, degrees of perfection, approach to or recession from perfection — with the same approach we employ with existence, namely, that something either is or is not, or is or is not now, something is either perfect or not, a principal meaning — namely, that of hierarchy — will vanish. And yet, we are told by the mystics, there are *degrees* of perfection in the soul and its spiritual life, and creatures can approach God, indeed to the point of "identity." Before these sayings can be adjudicated, they obviously must be understood. Our present school-metaphysics offers little by way of help. And yet the lost ideas are more or less recoverable by a recourse to common sense, which employs these ideas regularly. Metaphysics rooted in common sense, and the phenomenological reflecting upon them, has a chance, then, of reanimating something important, even when those common-sense meanings reappear in somewhat bizarre and technical disguise.

"Essence" and "existence" naturally are not the private property of metaphysics; their common equivalents are simply what something is, and that or how it is. Let us look first into the what of things, their nature, character or very essence. But for this discussion, it must be understood; we must, in effect, bracket as much as possible any particular views as to what any one thing itself might be, or indeed any real hypothesis as to what the ultimate terms of that description must be. We should therefore abstain from commitments about their physical essence, about the most useful contemporary scientific hypothesis about space, time, energy, and their particular universe; it is not to deny these hypotheses but simply to avoid tying our rather general remarks down to today's theories. For examples, then, and purely as examples, we shall revert to common sense; yet we should hope the same points could be illustrated by any hypothesis whatsoever about the nature of the objective world.

And so then how does the world turn its face to us initially, and even perhaps finally? Surely not everything we encounter — or experience or make or do — is on the same plane. The natures of some things are higher than those of others. But indeed, what is the height in question? More likeable, more agreeable, more moral? Or perhaps these valuations are derived from the very essence of the apparent things themselves? The attempt to explicate the initial sense of "higher" will now occupy us, but not in any literal sense. Any literal explication of higher would immediately implicate us in a specific metaphysics; we are therefore trapped, but not if they are understood only as being within a system; equivalent explications could be developed, *mutatis mutandi*, within others.

To anyone, the inorganic is lower than the plants growing out of it. Is that because we eat the plants but scarcely bother with the inorganic, except to breathe the air, drink the water, and salt our food? But even the most primitive man knows better, and would be more or less insulted to be reduced to this crass utilitarianism. Recently, an anthropologist asked a Tasaday in the Philippines: "Do you talk to the rocks?" The Tasaday replied, "No, do you?" Plants then appear as higher, higher than the rocks and stones because they are alive; if stones are worshipped, it is only by endowing them with the meaning of being alive, the temporary abode of a spirit. Taken as dead, they are not worshipped, but ignored as mere things. Life, even if only the minimal life of vegetation, is higher; both the living and the non-living obviously exist; but the essence of plants is higher than that of stones, and since their essences are different, in the higher there is a development of or growth out of. And since the plant is at least corporeal, but at most — and in addition — living, nourishing itself, reproducing, and healing itself, it begins to take on the aspect of an individual maintaining as best it can its own individuality, reacting and responding to its environment as an individual. A handful of earth is hardly an individual in any such sense; a drop of water in the lake? Is it anything at all? And to proceed through the familiar hierarchy: animals — leaping about, eating, making love, perceiving, remembering, and watching one another — simply make evident to any eye that now we have an essence higher than that of the plant. It is more lively, more independent of its environment, more purposive, in a word more of an entity, something *selbstständig*, more actual. The more independent the animal is, the more cunning, the more resourceful, independent of its environment, exploiting it, the more alive it is, the higher it is, the more noble, indeed the more like ourselves. They might even be our ancestors, in primitive views — as indeed they are for anyone; does not everyone have his totemic animal, whether confessed or not? They are holy and not to be senselessly killed without committing sacrilege, and if for food, then indeed eating takes on something of a sacramental character.

And then ourselves! Looked at quite objectively, are we not obviously the most alive, the most individual, the most free beings we can experience? If some imagine the self-dignifying of man to be nothing but a pathetic egotism, then the hatred of the human essence or its degradation, down to the ontologically lowest level of the inorganic, is on the contrary a sacrilege of the almost highest order, a reversal of the hierarchy of being. Such an egalitarianism despises the order of being which culminates in that most perfect being which reciprocally ordered the whole affair.

Some reflections upon this somewhat common-sense hierarchy of being may explain what is involved. If a drop of water in the pond, a handful of sand, or a wisp of smoke seem to be "beings" only by convention, artifice or courtesy, hence, in and of themselves, on the edge of not being beings at all, when a being appears to have an activity *of its own* it begins to appear alive — that is, to be something in and of itself. It distinguishes itself from its circumambient medium by that action, and to that extent is *a something*. And what is it, but that which acts. If mere inorganic movements appear wholly accountable by the movements impinging on the thing, the inorganic thing itself appears dissolved into its environing medium. But action, employing these movements, nevertheless gives to them its own goal; action is purposive, oriented to an end given it by the living agent. Thus, as we proceed up the hierarchy of beings, we find they are spontaneously accredited with life and being the more deeply they manifest categories like independence, action, freedom. But then what are these categories but precisely those which are attributed *par excellence* to absolute reality, that which is without qualification independent, actual, and free, and whose "life" is the eternal creation of the universe? This approach to absolute reality is not taken here as a proof, although it is sometimes so used: it is employed here only to give sense to very common appreciations of a hierarchy of essence or nature. What began as an intimation or conviction that not everything encounterable within our common experience is encountered on the same ontological plane, ends with the insight that the hierarchy is indeed ontological in essence and has nothing whatsoever to do with our desires, tastes or imagination. We do find ourselves at the top of the world, but this is more of an objective reading of matters than sheer anthropocentricity.

And if so far we have looked at generically different yet related types, it is hardly surprising that, when we reach the human essence, a distinctive modification occurs: if independence, freedom, and actuality are the marks we have been using to express "higher" and "lower," these all point to what is also evident from our common-sense reading of things. With ourselves, the highest is hardly the genus human at all, but the individual. The mind or spirit is highest when it is most individual, most free, most actual: it therefore manifests itself most evidently in those acts which are freest, most its own, hence most singular, and which take it to the highest awareness of its own spiritual life. Kierkegaard, Jaspers, and Heidegger might be quoted in support but their support would only support what has been almost universally granted anyway: that the spirit is most clear in heroism, genius, and sanctity — no matter how those terms are explicated, each of which names an excellence which is ontological, is unique, unrepeatable, and which to some eyes weds the eternal with the temporal for a time. For Kant, the "moral law within and the starry sky above" properly inspire awe; and the moral law within postulates God, immortality, and freedom, a postulate necessary for morality but unprovable as fact to objective reason.

So much by way of explaining a certain common-sense reading of experience as hierarchical in character or essence; it is seen as hierarchical insofar as the essence in question approaches what common sense also takes to be divine: actual, free, and eternal life. That hierarchy could be explained in any number of ways, and that given informally here could be more literally stated and argued for within systems as diverse as those of Aristotle and Hegel.

Essence is most usually contrasted with existence, the mode of being of the nature, essence or character in question. Modes of being are most usually distinguished into the possible, actual, and necessary. How then do we explicate these modes of being into "perfection"? Are they not all perfect, each being what it is? But no, a phenomenological clarification of what these terms intend does not show that each is on the same footing as the others. Possibility is usually taken as the self-consistent, that which lacks within itself contradiction. If it is self-consistent, then it is possible being, it could be. A square circle cannot be; a round circle could be. But, at the start, this announces that possibility bears an inherent reference to actual being; it is what could be actual, whether it is actual or not being left open. Leibniz even refers to a certain "straining" toward actuality among his domain of possibles and compossibles. And so all things actual are of course also possible; but perhaps not all things possible are actual; the "perhaps" is added to avoid metaphysical questions unnecessary for our present purpose. The *actual* is what simply is without further qualification. The further qualifications, is, was, will be, we take to be modifications of the simple untensed *is*. That something is might be taken to be a simple, unanalyzable fact, but clearly — for anything we can encounter in experience, whether it is or not — is not itself an unanalyzable fact but immediately discloses a new aspect: it is only if other things are, each of which equally depends upon other things or events, not itself. In a word, each existent actuality has its existence only upon the pleasure of other existences. Each therefore is, as an actuality, contingent upon other existences and can be only if they are. It cannot be in independence of them or in some logical vacuum. So far, then, existence or actuality implies a state of contingency or dependence. Finite, contingent existences cannot be ontologically perfect. In and of themselves, they have no complete or finished mode of being; they are needy of others.

The *necessary*, on the other hand, is that which cannot not be; it therefore is not contingent upon other things, but in and of itself must be. Nor is it a mere possible being; a necessary being is that whose mere possibility assures its actuality. Its being therefore is self-sufficient in every sense. Such a mode of being is by tradition assigned to *absolute being*, which is not merely a possible being, nor merely a being which happens to exist and might very well not be at all dependent upon other things, but which in and of itself necessarily and eternally is. At least necessary actuality is one feature of absolute being, and we shall leave open for the present whether it is the only feature. For our only present point is that the various modes of being have themselves a hierarchy of perfection, and in their internal meaning point to one another: possibility is possible actuality; actuality fulfills possibility but in itself is contingent upon other actualities, hence imperfect; necessary actuality is either that whose possibility assures its actuality or that actuality which is always and under all circumstances possible, an actuality which is of its own essence eternal.

The developed sense, then, both of essence and existence, what a thing is, and how it is, point in the same direction. What is meant by absolute being is that which is necessarily actual, which therefore is independent in essence and being of any other thing, which therefore is free of determination by any other thing. It is therefore perfect in essence and existence or being. And some such considerations are at least essential ingredients in most traditional definitions of absolute reality or God.

One further point should be noted in the present connection. The absolute reality under discussion is absolute in every respect. We have considered it under a few abstract notions: its "independence," its "eternity," its "necessity," etc. But then this represents only an arbitrary selection out of the infinite respects in which absolute reality can be contrasted with finite realities. Yet, again of its own essential nature, which announces of its own essence that it is "perfect," it is clear that what reason has in mind is no abstraction. Abstractions, literally, are parts taken away from a whole or universal aspects of a concrete. Abstractions cannot, in their character of being parts or aspects, have the absolute independence and reality which the essence of absolute reality defines. The concrete whole would always be more independent than some abstract part drawn from it. And so absolute reality in itself and in its essence, is, as Hegel emphasized, the most concrete of all. Even ideas such as "world" are themselves only abstract versions of absolute reality immediately raising a philosophical anxiety whether the world is indeed all, or about what lies beyond it, if anything, notions of other possible worlds or recesses within absolute reality which have nothing whatsoever to do with even possible worlds.

Now these considerations of what the essence of absolute reality demands are more unsettling for our phenomenology of mysticism. Could anyone pretend to have any such thing concretely before his mind or in his metaphysical experience when he uses the term *absolute reality*? Is the term not indeed as empty as the empiricists have always claimed? Is it not finally merely the barest, most pretentious claim to knowing what, on the surface of it, looks most unknowable? In a word, is it not merely what Kant thought he had shown about it, a mere *idea*, claiming to be knowledge which in principle no mortal mind can have? And if this empty idea — which claims concreteness but of such a sort that no reason could possibly have anything but a vanishing portion of it — is then larded out with the fantasies of hallucinated mystics, have we not reached the end of our discussion and proved, in effect, the opposite of what we desired to prove? But on the other hand, the idea of absolute reality has a certain unnoticed resilience, and perhaps there are resources within it which have not been fully explored. To wit, precisely what is the *mind* to which we deny the power of absolute intuition? It is indeed usually called *finite*, and while that looks comfortably modest, it may also be fundamentally wrong, although the error may demand exertions to be shown. Before giving up rational mysticism, then, as a hopeless project, we must direct our phenomenology to the mind itself, to the reason within, its essence, its necessary intentions, and its appropriate powers. This extension of our analysis also, and not by accident, coheres with the essence of our original goal, absolute reality. Clearly that essence must implicate every form of being; and one of the forms of being of most interest to our present question is mind itself. But were not the mystics among the first to declare the essential unity of mind and God?

Chapter III **Absolute Mind**

A. The Ego and Its Surrogates

Perhaps no term in the philosophical vocabulary is more subject to confusion than *I* along with its cognates and latinizations, such as ego, and downright opposites, such as my body. And yet the term *I* can originally have designated nothing remote from myself, nor a questionable entity subject to dispute but indeed that which is so close as to be identical with me, namely, I myself. No sooner, however, do I use the term, than I must involve myself in what frequently looks like the subtlest of investigations: I, *the* I, ego, the ego, self, the I myself, ego-ity, my soul, self-identity, person, personality, person-hood, *Dasein*, etc. ad infinitum. How complex and various the modifications and modalities of the subject can become is clear at a glance from Hegel's masterwork, *The Phenomenology of Spirit* as well as Husserl's beautiful *Cartesian Meditations*. With Husserl, the ego, while always retaining the same name, can construe itself in some four or five different senses; for Hegel the number has never been counted, since every dialectical development on its objective side correlates with a corresponding development on the subjective side. For our own purposes here, however, perhaps Descartes' *Meditations* would be the most useful of all. We cannot here be concerned with every mode of subjectivity but are looking for ourselves in each self's absolute purity, that is, divested of all that is *not* itself. And it is certainly not by accident nor for rhetorical or literary effects that Descartes proceeds by way not of deduction or objective proof, but rather by way of meditation. That is, neither the problem of Descartes, nor our own which is comparable, nor its resolution can be understood except on the terrain of the thinker meditating. Meditation, in this connection, is a first-personal reflection by the self upon its self. And such first-personal reflections re-enacted by each thinker are at the same time the basic attitude which (with other modifications) constitute the phenomenological method of Husserl. In any event, an effort to circumscribe the meaning of what we shall be discussing is clearly called for.

If I myself should ever become problematic to myself, I have only to reflect, meditate, or perform the phenomenological act of *divestment* to recover myself for myself. I then ignore in thought or "bracket out" that in my thought which is *not* me. This act of divestment or, mystically speaking, of purification, is not, needless to say, a factual or existential dismemberment of that factual solidarity of consciousness and its objective concerns which constitutes the intentional life of the ego accidentally related to its world. But the ego is only accidentally related to anything in its world, whether perceived things, projects to be accomplished, its past life, or ideal objects of mathematical or logical thought; otherwise, if it were essentially related to them, it could never have any temporal experience of them, come upon them by surprise or discovery, and its own conscious life would be staring at a network of the *a priori*, fixed forever in eternity. But, for contrast, the self *is* essentially related to itself, being identical to it; and since its relation to anything objective is accidental to it, but its relation to itself essential, it always has the opportunity for distinguishing itself from anything whatsoever which may appear to it in its world.

The process of divestment must be carried out with absolute rigor. The distinction between consciousness and various objects in the world is relatively easy; Descartes uses the method of doubt, for their existence can one and all be denied. Can it not all be a dream, or produced by autonomous dis-

.

turbances in the body? But still, one may say, they remain as
dreams, imaginations or perceptions of unknown origin. Absolute divestment demands a further step; the divestment of
the thinking ego itself from all that is not itself, and that
would include its own phenomenal world, as well as those
conscious acts which present that world to it. I think, perceive, dream, feel, but I *am* not those various acts in time;
rather I am that ego which now thinks, now perceives, now
remembers or dreams. These acts are indeed mine, and mine
most intimately, yet they are not me, nor am I composed of
them, nor their unity, nor anything else than myself.

The essential absurdity of supposing the transcendental
ego to be composed out of its own intentional acts is fairly
close to the mystical absurdity of supposing God to be a result
of, composed out of or analyzable into His own creatures.
Could Spinoza's *Natura naturans* be composed out of the very
modes of that substance? Or eternity composed out of time?
And so the various acts of the ego are precisely that, and
those acts can neither be nor be thought of except as modes
of the eternal actuality of the transcendental ego. It could only
be the most naive and incoherent empiricism which would
imagine that it would begin with "psychological facts" of common life, hoping to end with a clearer notion or even refutation
of the very transcendental ego which is their origin and active
source. The cure for this ontological and phenomenological
absurdity is nothing more than to accept Descartes' invitation
to his reader to meditate, by reflection to recover the simplest
and most certain of all truths: I think therefore I am; and
what am I but a "thinking substance," i.e., a transcendental
ego, transcendent to anything in the world, the world itself,
as well as its own stream of conscious life? The one thing the
ego is not transcendental to is itself. I am then neither a thing
in the world, the world itself, something to be accomplished,

nor my determinate perceptions, dreams, imaginations or thoughts; I am simply myself, and if this sounds unenlightening, it would be so only for those who wish to explain the ego by categories and descriptions drawn from the world or from logic, in short from every domain which the self is not. Meanwhile I cannot in principle be hidden from myself, though indeed I can in fact lose track of the whole problem and say anything I please. In short, I am the one possible being whose being is to be knowable.

I am, then, that which I am; and what I am is to be thoroughly transparent to myself, such that there never can be a doubt about the matter. I can doubt the existence or even the essence of anything which is not me, since to whatever extent it is not me, it presents to me an opacity. It is that phenomenological opacity which announces to me that it is indeed objective to me, and is not myself. It may indeed be secretly connected with something secretly connected with myself — by way, for example, of the body; but we are not discussing the secret constitution of things, that which is not phenomenal, or available to intuition, but precisely that which is so available, and hence can have no secrets, the autophenomenal ego.

If now I am to ask myself what I am, considered as I am phenomenologically for myself, I must be in a position to know. And if the answer seems too simple to be anything but disappointing, in the end it will not be, but rather disclose what Husserl calls "the wonder of all wonders." It is exactly what we started out looking for, namely, *I myself*. To ask further is, I think, superficially profound, but at the same time profoundly superficial; a little more inquiry reverses the question: what indeed is everything else? It is the enormous and confused class of everything else which is thought to be well-known but which in fact is not, that is the source of the question, what am I. The rational-mystic termination, then, of the question as to what I am in transcendental purity and divestment is found by noting that, for the question itself to have any sense, we must have been guilty of a deep misunderstanding at the start: an assumption that what is *not* I is clear to me. I then must try to find a category drawn from the not-I to answer the question as to what I am! Failing to find any such category, I then imagine that I am an enigma to myself, surely the maddest argument one could devise. And if "I am I" seems like a perfectly useless tautology, it must be understood that its function is not explanatory or descriptive at all, but indicative of an act by which the ego recuperates in explicit thought what it always was implicitly anyway refusing to budge from the self-evident.

And next, for ulterior purposes, it must be remarked that the identity of *I am I* when transferred to objective things that are not I, as in phrases such as "the sun is the sun," in their self-identity and tautologous character express nothing but existence reduced to possibility, equivalent to "a centaur is a centaur," or a "unicorn is a unicorn." But in the present case the expression *I am I* expresses both the essential identity of myself with myself as well as the actuality of the identity so expressed. As Descartes had it, I cannot doubt the existence (here, actuality) of myself any time I reflect upon my thinking; *what* I am thinking may indeed be doubtful, but that I the thinker am, in principle cannot be doubted by the thinker himself. And, of course, this is the thinker insofar as he is a thinker, and not insofar as he may also exist in the natural or physical world. I myself, then, am not in the same epistemological position to myself as I am to any other object whatsoever which I can perceive, think or encounter. I am not a hypothetical entity, an *ens rationis,* a universal concept, a word, nor an emptily entertained intention. In this one instance, the self in recuperating itself achieves an ontological and epistemological rock-bottom, beyond which it cannot go, nor would there be any phenomenological sense in attempting to go beyond it.

B. Expressions and Descriptions

1. Identity of ego: Since the ego is a primordial identity, the first conundrum is how anything can be identical with itself. This question resolves itself into what each might possibly mean by finding himself, each and every one, identical with himself! If the relation "identity" is understood externally, as it most habitually is, as two things or terms, each of which is then said to be the same as the other, clearly we are understanding the ego in the most absurd fashion possible; the ego was never anything but one in the first and last place. From where did the duality come, which then later is denied by the very sense of identity? If the identity is held to subsist between two linguistic terms, then it is not primarily predicated of the ego at all, but rather of linguistic designations of it, and the identity thereby loses its referential force. The only relevant sense of identity, then, when applied to the self cannot be that of external relation between two me's, each of which is then seen to be the same, but understood in the manner of internal relation. Here there is no distinction between factors later said to be the same, but where they are the same in the beginning and end, that is, there never was a distinction at all. The term *identity*, then, has a strictly negative force, denying difference of any sort whatsoever within the transcendental ego. The ego, then, is internally reflexive, and its so-called relation to itself is nothing but an expression of the fact that the self in question exists wholly on the level of consciousness or awareness or knowledge;

therefore, it is not exclusively knowledge of something else but inherently *self*-consciousness. Its being is its awareness, and that is what a self is. In other epistemological situations, it distinguishes itself from what it knows, "objectifies" the content of its awareness as a something or other not itself.

2. *Conceptualization and Judgment*: With such an entity in mind, that which each is, or rather, I am, the next question is how or whether it may be conceptualized, and what sense judgments about it must have. Clearly the language of the first person singular is not readily assimilable to that of the third person singular or plural. And if assimilated, that assimilation conceals within it a logical deformation which must be clarified unless hopeless paradoxes are to be generated.

A concept is, of course, the concept *of* something. For Kant, it belonged to the class of representations *(Vorstellungen)* by which something was presented to the mind as a universal or type. The representation was certainly not what it represented, but re-presented it under certain formal and universal conditions of representation in general which the transcendental unity of apperception required for perception or judgment. Hence the cognitive powers of mind were confined to dealing with its own representations, representations which to be sure owed something to the thing being represented, (the *Ding an sich*), but of which it could know *a priori* only those formal conditions of representation proceeding from itself. And to some extent, the same holds for the British empiricists, who considered the fundamental data of cognition to be impressions; our nature had impressed upon it certain modifications of its nature, which proceeded from an external stimulus, largely regarded again as unknowable, as indeed it must be in this schema.

The essential question which then emerges is whether the mind, or in our present case, the self, can grasp itself. Would it not have to have an impression originating *from* itself *upon* itself, in which case the real self, the origin of the impression, still remains unknown by that very self itself. For Kant, the answer is unequivocal. The soul, to know itself, must have a representation of itself, which like all representations must conform to the formal conditions of representation set by the soul in its cognitive capacity. In either case, the sad result is the same. I have no possibility whatsoever of grasping or knowing myself immediately, or intuitively. I have nothing but an assortment of impressions or representations among which I mysteriously acquire a suspicion that one is indeed myself, at least myself as I impress myself, or myself as I must represent myself. I become in principle inaccessible to myself, a stranger whose identity with myself must be accredited by external, hypothetical, and at best problematical credentials; and in any event, the I I *do* pretend to intuit, or grasp without concept or mediation, remains unknowable in essence. I am subject to a transcendental illusion. Now all of this in its overarching schema is wholly at variance with other philosophical schemata, among which is that of Descartes, for whom reason was not merely discursive but also intuitive. Its object need not be either an impression or a representation, but might in certain definable cases be the thing itself, the *I think*.

Now if the representative theory of knowledge has good use among a large body of concepts and judgments about external things, it does not follow that that schema is of universal validity. It fails precisely on the question of how the self apprehends itself, whether intuitively or whether it too must be classed as a case of representational cognition. Our present conclusion, to state it at once, is that the schema is hopelessly and incorrigibly wrong in the case of self-knowledge, as well as in the case of God considered in the ontological argument.

What phenomenologically we aim at is the sense of the self's immediate and intuitive cognitive unity with itself. It knows itself and knows that it knows it. And what it knows, itself, is indeed the self it knows. Any further self, hidden behind this phenomenological self, or posited as a stimulus for self-affection in order for it to make an impression upon itself — all that simply lies outside the question, which is what the self does apprehend and not what it does not apprehend. And indeed when that "soul" does finally emerge for Kant, in the *Critique of Practical Reason*, it can emerge only under the form of a *postulate* of practical, that is, moral reason. It is the immortal life of that postulated self, unknown to itself, in which the soul is supposed to take moral comfort; but then the nagging question returns, why should I take the least interest, moral or otherwise, in the fate of a me which is not the interested me and only hypothesized?

But perhaps one thing can be saved from this particular ship-wreck: for Kant, the very sense of the soul, though not its cognition, its freedom, immortality, as well as God, all emerged not through the representative knowledge of the first Critique, but in the moral volition of the second. Volition in turn is an act of the will, and not an object of scientific representative knowledge. And with this hint, we return to the problem. My cognition of myself, which is my self-identity, is not in the least by way of impressions or representations; it is intuitive and participational rather than representational, it grasps itself as it is; and the sense of what it intuitively grasps is not in the least assimilable to any objective representational sense without radical distortion.

If then I know myself by being myself and not by looking at myself, and if all conceptualization is by way of seeing a singular through the eyes of a universal under which it is subsumed, we can conclude that the self does not and cannot conceptualize itself. It knows itself rather in being or participating in itself, and such participating intuition is leagues apart from any spectatorial cognition. The I primordially does not look at itself, nor is it in any position to form an objective concept of itself to itself. Which does not mean it is ignorant of itself, but simply that it does not know itself in this way. Again the appropriateness of Descartes' *Meditations*.

If categories are objective universals, the intuitive self-reflection of the self does not fall under categories. And if it is clear that such knowledge cannot be objective, it must be equally clear that it cannot be by way of universals. Certainly my primordial apprehension of myself apprehends me as me, an absolute singular. Is it not essential to the very intention of the term *I* that it designate the first-person singular? This singular, which is the ego, is not known through some universal "Ego," "self-ness," or any of their universal equivalents. Nor does it need any such universal terms to be a form of cognition; intuition intuits the singular, which is not nothing, and — contrary to Kant's dictum that intuitions without concepts are blind and concepts without intuition empty — what intuition intuits must necessarily have "content" or it would be the intuition of nothing, that is, no intuition at all. Further, if the self-intuition were blind, it taxes the mind to see how a blind intuition could later be subsumed under anything whatsoever. Or how the empty concept could fill itself with what was, in and of itself, blind.

Further, a distressing paradox emerges when anyone even attempts to universalize himself under the concept *I*. At that precise point, his own singular being, that which is most intimately himself as knowable essence, turns out to be not himself at all, but rather a universal equally the essence of an infinity of others. The self-conceptualizer has lost himself in the concept, and therefore that concept may far better be called false than true. But then how can we speak? Not at all, meaningfully, if speech were dependent upon objectification or universalization. But happily it isn't, and we can now permit ourselves to speak as we would anyway, even if we had never heard of these bizarre theories. I saw the sun, I wish to eat, I hope for the better, I think therefore I am. All of these sentences, far from objectively describing anything, or describing them via universals, describe nothing whatsoever, but express the acts of the singular first-personal singular I, which lives, breathes and has its being in first-personal singular acts. Indeed, in and of itself, each I is pure actuality. It participates in this actuality and expresses that participation every instant of its life, to the perfect comprehension of everybody except the holders of eccentric theories. Curiously, in this domain, the essence of the singular is located in its singularity, and not in some universal it may also, accidentally, exemplify.

C. The Absolute Fracture

The previous discussion has led to the view that the infinitive *to be* suffers a radical split in meaning when specified to "I am" and "it is." The "am" expresses the mode of being of myself as I am to myself, identical with myself, and as I intuitively participate in myself and my acts of consciousness; and since I am in no sense objectifiable to myself or essentially characterizable by a universal concept, my being accordingly is in no sense analogizable to the kind of entity which is inherently objective and inherently knowable through the universal; "I is," therefore, is minimally a grammatical error, and maximally an ontological absurdity; needless to say, it is a grammatical impossibility because it is an ontological absurdity. And if we follow Descartes in re-enacting *cogito ergo sum,*, we do not agree that this meditation proves the existence of the thinking substance, if "existence" is taken as univocal in meaning to its application to anything at all which could be objective to that ego. The being of the self is only accessible to that very self, and any expression which expresses the being of the self is from ground up metamorphosed when transferred verbally to derived descriptions or affirmations of the being of anything at all objective.

Further, since I am myself, the sense of being expressed in "am" not only is but must be radically clear to me, whereas the intent of the term "is," as applied to objects for me, is and must remain obscure, measured against the radical clarity of "am." Thus while each knows perfectly well what it is to be himself, no one knows or can know what it is to exist as a thing. Indeed, virtually every explication of what existence means as applied to objects simply reverts to a long-winded formula which expresses what its existence might mean for us: a permanent possibility of experience; a source of surprise or shock (to us); that which we can quantify or measure; that which is a referential identity throughout various possibilities of expression; etc. And indeed some such thing is what objective existence means for us; what it is in and for itself remains either obscure or at bottom senseless. In answer, therefore, to the partisans of objective existence with its supposed clarity, against which the subjective expression of being is taken to be hopelessly obscure and difficult, raising frightful problems in both logic and epistemology, we can only remark that the shoe is on the other foot. The sober truth is that *I am* is inherently and absolutely clear to the I which meditates or reflexively grasps itself, whereas the existence of nothing objective whatsoever has any but a derived, provisional and, at bottom, unintelligible sense. This reversal of the standard of clarity and intelligibility occurs analogously in every thorough metaphysical system.

If with Plato the fundamental contrast or fracture is between *being* and *becoming*, it is not being as an abstraction from becoming — some sort of thinned-out image or an event which lasts an indefinitely long time — which is taken to be obscure; it is becoming itself which cannot be rationally understood, although it *can* be encountered. However, what is encountered is not thereby understood, but only encountered as an *other*, whose entire sense it owes to whatever participation in or imitation of being it may provisionally have or be thought to have. Similarly, as I remarked above, in the system of Spinoza, substance itself is the only thing of which we could possibly have an adequate idea; the mode is a mode of substance, not something intelligible in and of itself; it is nothing in and of itself but wholly modal in its essence and existence. Sense experience then, through which the transcendental ego encounters that which is not itself, when taken by itself is in principle the domain of obscurity, hypothesis, and estrangement. To reverse this relationship and pretend to find a clarity in what is essentially unclear — "clarity" now meaning "familiarity" — and to suppose that the expressions of the transcendental ego are strange, lacking in objective meaning, unverifiable, and probably best dispensed with altogether, is surely one of the greatest philosophical blunders imaginable. And this barbarism, it need hardly be repeated, is merely one form of the radical misunderstanding mystics themselves perpetually run into when their lucidity is declared to be nothing but euphoric raving; who indeed is raving?

D. Uniquely Subjective Expressions

If the sense `of "to be" is originally fractured into "am" and "is," corresponding to the modes of being appropriate to the I and to any object for that I, we might begin to suspect that the entire vocabulary of metaphysics is equally fractured. Inattention to the radical difference of meaning in terms, otherwise applied indifferently to the subjective or objective, can only lead to paralogisms and puzzles which cannot be resolved on the level on which they are posed.

   1. Singularity. The singularity and uniqueness of the ego for itself is identical with its primordial self-apprehension and being as a self. On the other hand, singularity applied to some objectivity for me degenerates into the task of characterizing something through a property or set of properties shared with no other actual or possible object. That such a comparison can never be completed empirically, demanding an impossible survey of an indefinite domain, is obvious. That singularity is attributed to objects *a priori* already announces the meaning of singularity in the transcendental ego, which has drawn that meaning out of its own depths, and as originally expressive of its own essence. Transferred to the objective, what was intuitively evident now becomes an empirical task of infinite and impossible proportions to be fulfilled only through hope. What could be more evident than that I know, directly and without inference, that I am not another? Or that I am not a universal? Is not each self a primordial self?

   That the so-called ego-centric particulars, this, here, now, all derive from the ego itself has been elegantly demonstrated in Asher Moore's essay "The Center of the World*." And the same is true of singulars designated by the definite article

---

*Asher Moore, "The Center of the World," *Boston Studies in the Philosophy of Science* 3 (1964/66).

"the," as in "the world." The singularity combined with uniqueness implied by the "the" could not conceivably be derived from a sense impression or datum; no one has ever or could ever experience the world; it is clearly a meaning drawn from the singularity and uniqueness of the ego as it experiences itself, but now given an objective sense.

2. *Substantiality*. The notion of substance is in the same boat. Taken as "that which exists in itself," and therefore not as a property of something else, a mode, phase, position, situation, quality, etc., of something else — there could be nothing whatsoever which could be a finite object for me which would offer that sense to me if I had not already gotten its sense from my very ego, the one primordial thing which is grasped by itself as an absolute, as that which is not a property of some other thing. Provided with that idea, the thinking ego can then discuss with itself what particular objective candidates are suitable for the designation, if any, and in what particular derived or degenerate mode. Naturalists most usually find no individual thing absolutely substantial, thus transferring substantiality in its final sense to the natural world itself, a concept we shall later show to be *a priori* and derived from the source of all these meanings, the ego.

3. *Freedom*. That the ego experiences itself as free could hardly be denied and seldom is. What is denied, of course, is that this experience is proof that it really is so. Our present question is solely that of meaning, and our contention is that this meaning has its primordial and essential source in the ego itself; the ego experiences itself as free from anything not itself and free for whatever it chooses. So much is the simple, phenomenological datum, confirmable by anyone. For Kant, as we mentioned, it is a postulate of the moral will. If now that meaning is attributed to objects for me, the so-called problem of freedom arises, and that it is a problem only con-

firms our present diagnosis that the subjective sense, when regarded as a property of objects, undergoes such a radical shift of meaning that what is then literally thought, a free object, is itself senseless. Now if the object in question is my person, looked at as an object either by me or by another, for one thing it is no longer mine, nor a person, nor anything which could have the property "freedom" at all. Freedom so objectified turns out to be an objective movement without a cause, a spontaneity or occurrence without sufficient causes external to the thing moving, hence a sort of "indeterminism." Now our question is not whether or not there are any such insufficiently determined phenomena, but rather even if there were, whether any such thing is what is meant by the primordial sense of freedom, namely that which I directly intuit in myself. Objective freedom now applied back to myself as spontaneous movements of the soul, arising from nowhere and aiming at nothing, would be regarded by that ego as monstrous phenomena and not the glory of life. And if freedom is necessarily one of the conditions of responsible, moral action, uncaused motions attributed to the soul would be nothing but an absolute and uncontrollable irresponsibility and indeed madness. When my actions appear to me uncaused, that is, when I am not the cause, then I have no alternative but to regard them as only apparently uncaused, but really the result of a hidden objective cause, namely, pathological connections of my body or soul. My actions, then, are properly regarded as something for which I am not responsible, hence not actions at all; my spiritual house is now invaded by foreign agents. I would seek treatment to restore my body or soul to freedom from such agents and for personal responsibility. Along these lines, Spinoza argues that freedom is nothing but ignorance of the causes. And yet this violently conflicts with our sense of freedom properly drawn from ourselves; when I freely and responsibly choose, it is far from the case that I act in ignorance of the causes; quite to the contrary, in those cases and those alone I have certainty that I know the cause: the cause is myself, such that it would be preposterous to look elsewhere. Freedom, then, is an expression deriving only from the ego's self-awareness, and properly attributable only to that ego's own acts and mode of being. And not surprisingly, the customary objectification of freedom into things in the world (excluding the hypothesis of indeterminate quantum leap) most easily finds no single finite object free at all. If objective freedom is to be found anywhere, it will be only at the end of objective finitude, namely in the world as a whole which, since it is a whole, might accept the predicate freedom; there being nothing else outside it, it must be through its own laws self-determined, that is, free. Or else, not free, since as a whole it is thought of as a "machine" or at best, an "organism" obeying the laws of its own nature. These cosmological questions are not our present interest; what is to the point is that freedom is not an objective category, but solely a subjective expression; any transference of it from its home source to a problematic realm of objective events or things loses its original sense and provides only unintelligible surrogates.

4. *Property.* That things have properties, and indeed the very meaning of thing as that which can have properties, is obvious enough; but then again, what precisely is the sense of property? That sense already has its own proper meaning in the domain of subjectivity. Property is what is mine, and objective properties are what are its. But how can any object whatsoever properly own anything, hence claim it as its property? Logically, a thing has a property if the proposition which says it has such and such a property is true. All of which is itself true enough and yet misses our present question, to wit,

the primordial and proper sense of truly owning at all. Objectively construed, the relation is a bare externality; the thing has its properties, or it is true that the thing is qualified such and so. In short, the connection between the thing and its properties is taken as either just so, or that the synthesis between them is actually in the proposition which states the fact. But the genuine notion of property is surely an internal one; the relation between me and my acts is never an external relation; they are mine because I did them, or — as Hegel puts it — I determined myself to them. What then is mine is what I properly do and claim. If then I call my body mine, it is precisely because it responds to my will and choice, therefore is animated by my freedom and expresses that freedom. If it did not, as when a limb is paralyzed, then I hardly know it as mine. The language, then, of "property" and possessive "mine" derive straightforwardly from the ego's own consciousness of itself, not from external observation; and when transferred across the subjective-objective fracture, can only appear as a peculiar, external relation between an object and its properties; and yet the externality of the objective sense of property is exactly what property in the first place was designed to remove. Nothing is more internal to me than myself and mine. All other things are not mine, and appear as such phenomenologically.

It is not our intention here to run through one by one the entire categoriology of objective metaphysics, an impossible and futile task. It is sufficient to note that in fact objective metaphysical categories are nothing but decomposition products of the consciousness of the ego of itself; extrajected upon the external world, we arrive at ideas which taken purely objectively are absurd, and which taken only half-way through are mish-mashes of the objective and subjective. The mystical ego, confident that it is indeed reality in its pre-eminent sense and at the same time the source of all meanings which can be meaningful to it, would never think of finding itself problematical and the world clear; it knows which way things lie, and that it itself is indeed "the wonder of all wonders"; but then while indeed wonderful, not opaque. And so there would be no particular point in extending the analysis to terms such as "infinte," "absolute," "eternal." Each of these simply emphasizes one aspect of the transcendental ego, where it has its proper home; and if we proceed to employ the idea externally, we find ourselves either in absurdity or else simply construing the world itself as an objectified subject. Whatever intelligibility the world has derives strictly from the source of intelligibility, the ego transcendental to that world.

E. The Transcendental Ego and Its World

The burden of the immediately preceding remarks is simply that the transcendental ego is not merely intelligible to itself, but that it is the radical source of intelligibility of whatever presents itself to it as objective. The objective is not exactly coterminous with the "world," since there are many objectivities which are not ingredients in this world or any world, like propositions about the world, or indeed descriptive propositions about the ego itself. And yet it would be difficult to deny that the world occupies a very central place not merely in the life of the ego but in its perpetual temptation to objectify being, and finally to attempt the cardinal error of objectifying itself to the point of finding itself and its singular, absolute and transcendental freedom, unreal unless it can justify itself as a fact in that world. And so the world has a weight almost sufficient to undermine the conviction of the self that it is at all.

To lighten that oppressive weight to the point of zero, it

is sufficient to examine what the ego can possibly mean by "world," and what the source of that meaning is. The problem and its solution are not altogether unlike that of Samuel Johnson who, according to Boswell, once had a nightmare that he had been outclassed in witty conversation by an opponent; on awakening, he suddenly found relief from his depression by the simple realization that he also was the author of his superior opponent. My present point is not that the ego "makes" the world, but that it certainly makes its meaning; what the world may be without its meaning we must leave for others to say.

The term *world* has so many variants that it would require a separate treatise merely to enumerate them. Perhaps they can be ranged between two extremes: the physical cosmos at one end and the human world at the other. The physical world is generally thought of as devoid of our purposes, values, and ambitions; it is a system of objects and processes which proceed either at random, or by law, or by both, and may not be a system at all, and whatever it is, its more precise nature we must leave to the monthly reports of physicists and astronomers. It is an object of awe for many — including Kant, but not particularly for Hegel. The Psalmist felt it declared the glory of God. Pascal felt lost in it, hanging between two infinities, the infinitely large and the infinitely small. And while such sentiments play no direct role in contemporary theories, they do indeed guide the direction of thought of the theorist. Einstein rejected chance as an ultimate factor in the universe, saying God does not play dice with the world. For our purposes here it is not necessary to enter into these questions, except to notice that whatever the physical world is, it is not in any version whatsoever a possible object of perception. No one has seen it, touched it, heard it. How then can it have any meaning whatsoever for us, if perception is the origin of its meaning? And yet, every actual perception of particular things includes an implicit reference to the world. Perception believes that what it perceives exists until contrary evidence comes along and that "existence" is in that very imperceptible world. The fundamental "infinity" ingredient in the notion of world is not to be restricted to its extent or divisibility in either space or time. It is ingredient in every single thing taken to exist in the world. Such things, if they are real, are taken to be subject to an infinite number of perceptions, from an infinite number of perspectives, by a theoretically indefinite number of perceivers. These are all factors in the meaning of "a thing in the world." The notion of infinity, inherent in world, communicates itself to everything in the world; again, infinity is an essential ingredient in the meaning of world and its worldly or factual components, no matter how these are classified.

But then the transcendental ego has other resources for its own meanings than humble perception, let alone those "impressions" of Hume which never rise to the level of perception, although they furnish material for it. In short, the transcendental ego, already being infinite, has no need to receive the idea of world from the world itself, an impossibility in any case. Whether in fact the physical world is either infinite or finite Kant thought undecidable in principle; it could be argued and refuted either way. But, either way, there remained the idea of a world, suggested to us by the "starry sky above," but only suggested and not given as a datum. In any event, the physical world as an ultimate encompassing cosmos, is a correlate not of the senses but of reason; and reason itself is merely another name for one act of the transcendental ego. The world then, as a correlate of reason, is not the same thing as reason; it is reason objectified.

But then what would motivate reason to objectify itself,

or, put otherwise, why should the transcendental ego "posit" a world, to use Fichte's phrase? "Objectification" is recognition of what is not myself, the meditating transcendental ego. In no sense does anyone outside the madhouse imagine that he is the world; whatever else the world may be, it inherently, and of its own meaning, is that which is not myself; it is other to myself. And, dialectically, at this point two things are necessary: that what is not myself needs a me which it is not. Otherwise put, if the world were purely and simply a hieroglyph of reason, transparent to the bottom, even in principle if not in fact, it would no longer be anything recognizable as a cosmos. It would simply be me all over again, without check and restraint. And yet, it is that absolute *other* in which I live and out of which I die. On the one hand, then, the world must be other, and yet on the other hand that otherness also is possible only to that to which it is other. It is intelligible that there is an other to the ego; but that intelligibility does not make it intelligible in any other sense.

Within these considerations, that which motivates the transcendental ego to recognize its own other I believe must be called an arbitrary fact. The ego associated with its living body finds itself confronted with its other in experience; that general fact cannot be deduced from itself nor from reason. It simply is so. For some, it is a metaphysical irritant; for others a source of awe, wonder, and the singular delights and miseries of life. It is the world in which the transcendental ego has transcendentally chosen to live and in which it continues to live at its own option. It is also the ontological expression of the fracture discussed earlier between subjectivity and objectivity, reflected in the difference between a subjective expression and an objective description.

The world, however, in the range of its meanings is hardly restricted to the starry sky above or the infinitely small or infinitely perceptible. In short, and most commonly, world also means the human world, the world we live rather than that which we try to reconstruct by inference from observation. And now we are closer to home, to a world which is not the correlate of our reason, but rather of our hopes, ambitions, actions and defeats, our parents, lovers, friends, and enemies. In short, the transcendental ego is also the soul of a living body; it animates that body, its actions, its desires, its perceptions. Presiding behind every perception and every action, oblivious of its own operation is the transcendental ego. I perceive this and that, I do or refrain from doing this or that, and while this I is rarely explicitly conscious of its own constitutive role, and indeed could hardly perform its own acts if it were explicitly so conscious, nevertheless an analysis of all its acts reveals the eternal presidence of that ego. That the transcendental ego is itself eternal, whereas its actions and perceptions are temporal, need detain us for only an instant; there certainly is no need that every factor of a temporal process itself be temporal. To catapult the entire frame of conscious life into the categories of temporal life would turn the entire affair into an absurdity. For Plato, time is the moving image of eternity; but eternity is hardly another temporal event.

Both perception and action, two central factors constituting the human world, are unthinkable without the ego perceiving and acting, and are so presented to the least reflection upon them. The human world disclosed to action and perception, the world within which such activities take place and which they presuppose, is then an objective correlate of the embodied transcendental ego, the ego insofar as it animates its own living body. That the ego in its purity is not that body, whether the body be conceived as objective or as lived, i.e., already animated by the ego, has, I think, been sufficiently argued by Descartes, as well as Spinoza and Husserl. My own derivative version may be found elsewhere.* Suffice it to say, it will be presupposed here. Still, a few examples may serve to recall what is at issue.

I see this room. Or, to put it more accurately, I seem to see it; I don't wish to quarrel whether there really is such a room or whether I really am seeing it. For our purposes, it is enough to focus our attention on the whole affair as a phenomenon. At least the phenomenon is certain, if nothing else is; and the phenomenon is enough. But precisely what is this banal event? I am immediately aware of a three-dimensional room, full of people. The ordinary event of seeing a spatial object is itself an event of the most extraordinary sort. My object, spread out in three dimensions, all comes together into my perception of it, a perceiving which in and of itself is not spread out in three dimensions. That is, by my perception of it, it is assimilated or reduced to an act of perception, which in no way resembles its object. Neither I, the perceiving self, nor my act of perception is a three-dimensional object. Indeed if either I or my act of perception were themselves three dimensional, we would be faced with a pure absurdity: there would be within this room two rooms of equal size, the room I look at, and then I and my perception of it, now become another room occupying this very room. No, there is only *one* room! The ego and its perception of it is not a second room at all; and if it were, it could not perceive this room but only be another funny spatial object lying within the originally perceived room. In any event, what could be clearer than the fact that the *I perceive* is a non-spatial act, related to a spatial object, but not in and of itself spatial?

And so, as we explore the extraordinary character of the

*William Earle, *The Autobiographical Consciousness* (New York: Times Books, 1972), chap. 3.

I, the first thing perhaps to note is that it is not in the least spatial, hence certainly not physical at all. As I hope is apparent, we are trying to make plausible our view that the thinking ego is indeed a transcendental something or other, and therefore a fit candidate for its own mystic claim that it is identical with absolute reality or God. Our method, however, is not by fits and trances, with all due credit given to them, but by a somewhat patient exploration of mundane phenomena which anyone can verify.

But then, no doubt, the ego is in *time*? The word *time*, of course, means many things, and perhaps no one is very clear about what it means. But for our present purposes, let us take it as naming the very flux and flow of the world. I do not mean the obvious fact that some things are moving while others remain at rest. I mean that even for things clearly at rest for us, each moment of their rest is different from the next moment and from the previous moment, although the thing itself sits there with recognizably the same face. But the real time I wish to talk about is that Heraclitean flux which pervades the world like some ever-blowing wind. Again, the banal truth is that everyone is aware of this flux of time. Everyone knows at heart, even if we choose not to think of it, that the entire experienced world is some sort of ontological bonfire, forever consuming and forever renewing itself within the now. But then the odd feature of it all is that the I knows it immediately; what sort of thing, then, is the I which is aware of the fire? Is it too caught up in it, a participant in the fire, or is it something above the flames? Yet, is it not immediately clear upon reflection that nothing wholly and exclusively temporal could possibly be aware of time? Being itself wholly different at each moment, how could it apprehend this difference? How can anything wholly in flux be aware that it is in flux? To take another example, how is it possible to understand a simple sentence or a simple melody? A sentence is not understood until the last word has sounded, nor a melody until its last note, unless either is so conventional as to permit us to anticipate it. But then when the last word or note has sounded, the whole sentence and the whole melody is somehow present; that is, the words and notes at the beginning are retained at the end. And so what is no longer literally sounding in our ears must still be present in retention, or no sentence, no melody could appear to our mind. If then the ego itself did not preside nontemporally over these movements, in order to gather together at the end all that preceded, neither linguistic nor musical sense would be possible. That which can so preside over the flux, retain what was as past, but still retain it, obviously cannot be exclusively a temporal event itself. It is related to time but not itself temporal. The comprehension of the flux, then, cannot be itself exclusively an item in it. If the *I think*, the ego, then, is neither a spatial volume nor an instant in the flux, it is transcendental to both and discloses again something of what Husserl called the wonder of wonders. And yet, it is indeed ourselves, and not a hypothetical entity; it is closest to us, being identical with ourselves.

As for action, to and for itself, i.e., phenomenologically, the ego — acting, deciding, or simply consenting to act — is invariably aware of its own freedom to act; objectively it may raise questions about itself, but then it entangles itself with needless conundrums, which we have discussed earlier in this chapter under the title freedom. Indeed, few have ever questioned the intuitive awareness by the ego of its own sovereign independence. Kant regards it as a necessary hypothesis of the moral will, but not objectively knowable, as an event in nature. Freudians are ever suspicious that what the ego causes is in fact nothing but a concealed effect of the id and the unconscious. Marxian sociologists favor social determinism, and again the secret workings of economic class interest which they delight in unmasking. But indeed, the intuitive or participative consciousness of freedom is absolutely not reducible to the ignorance of anything, or the secret, unconscious influences of anything whatsoever; the consciousness of freedom is not an ignorance of causes, but a knowledge of causes; that knowledge is that *I myself choose*, hence I am indeed the cause and nothing external to my own ego can cause it to act. If then, through our perpetual fascination with the objective world, we ask: *what made you choose this rather than that?* we have simply misunderstood the original consciousness and its deliverances. Nothing but myself made me choose; and if one still asks why, the appropriate answer is invaribly that of offering a motive, a goal, or a purpose. In short, the reason is teleological, rather than by external, or efficient causation. But the teleological explanation to the question why, preserves the freedom of the ego; for have I not also chosen the goal? The goal or purpose can hardly be understood as a force drawing me thither, by analogy with magnetism, it owes its force to that ego which sets it as a goal.

The phenomenology of my awareness of other subjectivities has been given in exquisite detail by Husserl in the fifth *Cartesian Meditation.* and need not be repeated here.

The burden of the last portion of this present chapter is to indicate the presiding role in ordinary life as well as physical speculation of the same transcendental ego with which we began. The transcendental character of the ego is disclosed, then, not merely in and for itself in its radical reflection upon itself, in the Cartesian "I think therefore I am," but also and universally in every perception and every action of that ego. True, these perceptions and actions are the work of the transcendental ego in its association with the body, hence are not purely the work of the ego; nevertheless they are impossible without that ego, and this mysticism of everyday life might do something to alleviate the otherwise bizarre or even grotesque claims of the mystics themselves. All life is mystical, not merely a selected sample of ecstatic cases.

F. The Fracture Mends Itself

The absolute reality which we have considered in the second chapter, and as issuing forth from the ontological argument, first appears as an absolute essence which is not in the least "my idea," "my thinking," or in any way to be confounded with my representations. The onological argument defends an intuition of absolute reality — that of which every finite thing I encounter or could encounter is but a mode, delimitation, or indeed creation. It is, in short, an absolute object. Under the name God, the believer — or, in our case, the philosopher — who encounters such an absolute object, encounters God as the *absolutely other*. Rudolph Otto's *Idea of the Holy* has beautifully explored the phenomenology of this moment. And mystics of every stamp never tire of emphasizing in one stage the absolute remoteness of God, his impenetrability by our thought, the absolute diremption between any category we find intelligible and those proper to God. God is not real according to what we find real; he has no being, if being is what we encounter in this world. Neither has he determinate essence, and what we deem good may as well be evil or indifferent to him. In short, his being is wholly transcendental to our intellects and reason; and the essence of blasphemy is to be unaware of the heterogeneity of what is properly his and what ours. Best to cultivate the doctrine of learned ignorance. Ultimately the most rational act is to commit a suicide of reason, to reduce to abjection the pride of reason's pretention to know anything at all. Even for Descartes, the eternal truths grasped by reason are for God contingent upon His will.*

Unquestionably, all this makes sense. But the sense it makes carries with it a counter-sense; if it does make sense, to whom does it make sense, and how indeed is it possible for intuitive reason to intuit that which it maintains it cannot intuit? If there is shuddering and awe before the *mysterium tremendum*, that shuddering and awe draw their sense from the transcendental ego, as their intentional source. And so the transcendental ego does know that before which it lays down its finite conceptual tools. It knows it sufficiently well to know that its finite tools are wholly inapplicable. But then its whole resources are hardly exhausted by finite concepts and representations. If they were, there would be no shuddering and awe, no capitulation before the absolute, no insistence upon learned ignorance. In fact, there would be no problem for it at all; its problems would be strictly practical or finite, and, running along its merry way, it would never find — in the indefinite series of events and things — anything whatsoever to give it pause, except those finite problems which envisage nothing but finite solutions, whether yet found or not. In a word, the absolute diremption between the transcendental ego and God cannot, in the last analysis, be absolute; for if it were it could never be known, felt or even retain the slightest sense.

Our own analysis so far has insisted on something comparable. Being, we argued in the last chapter, is radically split in significance when applied to the subjective and to the objective. And yet in the intuition of God, the ego and its absolute object do indeed meet, on the plane of intuition. The

*Cf. Harry Frankfurt, "Descartes on the Creation of the Eternal Truths," *Philosophical Review* 86,1 (January 1977): 36-57.

act of intuition intuiting God is therefore itself a synthesis of the two. I am myself, and absolutely and eternally myself; God is Himself and absolutely Himself. At this point what could be said except that we have two absolutes, with little possibility of any relationship; in which case, neither could have the least relation or commerce, the one with the other. And the inevitable consequence, at least for us: that this very situation could neither be known or have any sense whatsoever.

The absolute fracture then cannot in the end be absolutely absolute, if the barbarism be permitted. There is then some need for a re-examination of the question. Maybe something has been overlooked. And perhaps what has been overlooked is that we have indeed constricted the original meaning of absolute reality or God by considering it as an absolutely other object. It naturally appears this way at first glance, particularly in the ontological argument, since the intent of that argument was to show the objective being of God; God was in objective reality exactly as the subjective intuition of Him intuited. God was not there as representation, idea, concept or anything which could be considered a figment of my imagination. The purport, then, was precisely to establish the objective reality of an infinitely perfect reality. All well and good; but then is it not precisely that objectivity which infected the very essence of God so established? God, as objective, cannot be absolutely absolute. "Objective" must imply objective-to, or, if taken as "independent," then independent-of; and with these expansions, we can perhaps see that we have surreptitiously given a limitation to the absolute reality originally intuited. Both phrases explicitly relate that absolute reality to something else, namely ourselves, by way of declaring that reality to be objective to us, or independent of us.

It is necessary, then, to remove this final limitation from what was originally intuited as absolute reality; it must, in other words, be intuited as for itself, and not as it is for us exclusively, or even in part.

And next, what is that which is absolutely for-itself, but the transcendental ego itself as it is for itself? Does it not immediately follow that the transcendental ego is God thinking Himself, the self-awareness of absolute reality? Spinoza has said that our idea of God is identical with God's idea of Himself, not that it was like God's idea, or referred to it, or a representation of it, but identical with it. Meister Eckhardt said, "I am God." The mending of the fracture, then, is in one additional intuition, that the inner being of the transcendental self is one and the same as God. Or, put otherwise, absolute reality subjectivized. And if the "subjective" has frequently been that which true philosophical or scientific thought should escape from, it is here regarded as the metaphysical fulfillment of various partial and provisional schemata which rest too soon on the logically abstract or on an objective, natural cosmos. Needless to say, the "subjective" in question is transcendental and not empirical or empirically existent; and yet it is what each of us *is* most intimately, in principle perfectly transparent, and behind which no one can go; nor could it make the least sense to wish to go further. Such is the wonder of all wonders.

No wonder then that the transcendental ego innately possesses such extraordinary powers and resources! No wonder the conviction of its reason that it has at least the roots of absolute truth, no matter how much it can wander. Or that its own reason is not merely a human power like the digestive faculty or walking on two legs. The truth is that reason, when in full reflexive consciousness of its own nature, has never called itself merely human reason, but has for reasons of modesty desisted from calling itself divine, although that is precisely what it is when it is itself. And it goes without saying that perhaps most frequently, when it imagines it is reasonable, it may well not be; but then we are talking not about the very essence of reason, but about certain performances which fall short of its ideal essence. And yet its essence is not to be a failure of itself.

Two extraordinary arguments, the ontological argument and Descartes' *cogito ergo sum,* have been sore spots in the history of philosophy. They are in effect uniquely stimulating and offensive to a certain relaxed empiricism. This chapter has endeavored to show their intimate and logical connection and some consequences of that connection: that reason itself is mystical, and that each transcendental I is God.

Chapter IV **Mystical Sources of Excellence**

The burden of the preceding discussion was to establish a few general points: that the transcendental ego is the source of the sense of whatever can appear to it; that common meanings, such as space, time, the world, and things in the world could not possibly appear in any form whatever except to such an ego; that the meaning *absolute being* or God, similarly, could not be meaningful except to such an ego; and that the only ego adequate to such tasks must indeed be transcendental and, in fact, the consciousness (in one aspect) of God Himself. It is therefore identical with God in one of His aspects. Simply put, the transcendental ego *is* absolute being *thinking*. Both absolute being and the transcendental ego are eternal; but "eternity" signifies eternal actuality or eternal act, hence never to be confused with any abstraction or static state, neither of which could possibly be. Time can be nothing but eternity taken serially, and a dead abstraction taken serially remains a sequence of states or moments none of which actually is, any more than a series of such states could be.

But now, for the present discussion, I should like to alter the vocabulary somewhat, without introducing any new ideas. For the cumbrous phrase *transcendental-absolute*, I shall substitute a series of terms deriving from "sacred"; and for its opposite, the "profane" or "blasphemous." If the sacred is within the temple, the consecrated, the holy, and the profane is what is outside the temple of the gods, either ignoring the sacred or scoffing at it, perhaps we shall have a vocabulary more suitable for the discussion of the topics which follow. According to the preceding discussions, the transcendental ego — or self — is, in its identity with absolute being or God, not merely within a temple: it is the very god of the temple.

But the entire scene is now enlarged to include a range of actuality far beyond the mere awareness of space and time, the world, and its perceived objects — which, after all, serve as a mere background for the activity and aspirations of the soul. A soul would have to be impoverished indeed to preoccupy itself with perception, with such perceptions, moreover, which it can hardly help having anyway, and whose analysis and clarification lead to nothing but the fairly obvious.

The eternal soul lives also temporally, while it does so, and lives therefore in what may be regarded as a paradox. The paradox however between its own assurance of its eternal life and its temporalizing of the same is not fixed forever, but dialectical, a polar tension between two claims. The activity of the soul, therefore, might just as well be regarded as a continuing resolution of what might otherwise seem to be a static hostility. This effort and achievement of resolution, the aspiration toward and accomplishment of excellence, will be interpreted in this chapter, then, as the preservation, enhancement, and celebration of the sacred, the god within each.

Traditional, indeed stale names for three domains of such aspirations are ethics, aesthetics, and logic, which devote themselves respectively to that famous old trio, the good, the beautiful, and the true. That a good deal of the philosophy of the twentieth century attempts to ground each of these studies on premises acceptable only to logical understanding — a logic moreover committed to nothing but the principle of non-contradiction, thereby avoiding "faith," "revelation," "creeds," etc. — hardly needs proof. It is indeed a hangover from the worst of the Enlightenment, and somehow has easily managed to skirt the whole magnificent sweep of thought of nineteenth century idealism, whether critical, as with Kant, or absolute as with Fichte, Schelling, and others through Hegel. This oversight itself has philosophical motivations which it is not part of our program to develop. Nevertheless, the oblivion into which idealism has fallen in the twentieth century, only very recently being partially corrected, is itself a premise upon which most positivism, pragmatism, scientism, and linguistic analysis rests. It is indeed a scandal, or put in our present terms, blasphemous. It aims to achieve a new clarity; what it has achieved beyond some questionable novelties remains to be seen, but certainly cannot be seen within the horizon of its own terms.

I hope it does not need to be emphasized that my concern here is hardly with anything that could be identified with any denominationalism, clericalism, creedalism, revelation, or faith, no matter how sympathetic it might be to these on other terms. It does concern itself solely with the deepening of reason itself to the point where reason, as the light of the transcendental ego, is understood to be identical with the divine, indeed a function of it, but that this reason has little to do with logical inference, deductive reasoning, or anything whatsoever that could be or wishes to be formalizable. It is precisely what even Kant denied: intuitive reason. The idea, therefore, of founding philosophical disciplines upon formal logic, or miscellaneous appeals to the "natural understanding," common sense, or science appear as nothing short of both absurdity and blasphemy. That they have, one and all, foundered into confusion and a proliferation of "considerations," articles, papers, and a squabble of arguments against arguments is not to be wondered at. That particular result was predictable from the beginning. Once the sacred center has dropped out of consideration, what could be left but incoherent and groundless ratiocinations multiplying themselves to infinity?

I shall then consider in turn three aspects of the sacred aspirations of the sacred soul: the good, beautiful, and true.

Each will be considered as a form of the ultimate celebration by the sacred of the sacred; nothing short of some such thing could possibly be either coherent, true, good, or beautiful.

A. The Ethical

The world into which we are born, in which we live, and out of which we die is haunted by the sacred. Indeed, it is constituted by the sacred, structured throughout by it, and therefore unthinkable without that category in its infinite manifestations. The "starry sky above" struck awe in Kant's heart, and the "heavens declare the glory of God" to the Psalmist. It is not, of course, that God Himself was a star, or all of them put together; if so, the heavens would have nothing to declare; God would be visible at last. Nor was God the law which described the movements of the heavens; for the Psalmist, that would have been nothing but regular motion in a circle, going on forever. This, of course, may be an inspiring thought to some, but it is doubtful whether such an idea was the inspiration for any psalm. In any event, wonder at the natural cosmos is natural, and expresses the instinctive metaphysical sensitivity of every man. The simple truth in all this is that the infinite natural cosmos, in which we are, is already the objective correlate of a transcendental idea, and not the object of any perception. All the objects of perception, the stars in this instance, are located within the cosmos, whose origin or principle is only declared by the stars, but never itself visible. And if it were visible, then we should have to understand another cosmos within which it was.

All of this is part of the human world, available and even insistent every night. Our daylight world looks profane and even tawdry in comparison. It is nothing but the shouts in the market place, the news of the newspaper, a certain blare and business, engrossing in its own way, yet surely not sacred. But then this first glance at what Heidegger calls, with his usual elegance, *durchschnittliche Alltäglichkeit*, itself begins to disclose more mysterious sides, upon even the least reflection. The daylight world of human beings, the world of activity within culture and civilization, the more explicitly human world, itself has some aspects which at first may be disturbing for any empiricist or any man of affairs but perhaps, when plumbed, may disclose that not merely do the heavens disclose the glory of God, but that glory also glares in the daytime. The burden of the present section is to show that not merely does the mystic and transcendental peep out in peculiar and disturbing times, but that it is indeed as constitutive of the human cultural world, the *Lebenswelt*, as "cosmos" is of what we see in the heavens. The other matter which struck awe in the heart of Kant was the "moral law within"; and again, traditionally, God is worshipped principally and most worthily in "the heart of man," in respect and love. And so we are led dialectically to examine the absolutely central and originating role of the mystical idea of absolute reality which is one with each man in the structuring and constitution of the social and cultural world in which we find ourselves. Our present theme, then, is the derivation of every ethical idea from the transcendental idea of *the absolute*, or, what is the same, *the Holy*.

"Ethics" of course derives from *ethos*, or custom, and perhaps that is our first encounter with what permits and what forbids. I may in some youthful euphoria feel I may do anything whatsoever; but then there are some things I discover which are not permitted; they have never been done without sacrilege, they are forbidden. That they are forbidden may give a new relish to their violation, a thrill and exhilaration, and to do them anyway will appear to me as an act of liberation. And yet, the thrill of liberation itself would be impossible unless I recognized also the forbidden character of what I am tempted to do.

Many of these taboos have to do with sex, with respect for one's elders and ancestors, respect for one's fellows in general, with proper speech, with restrained behavior. And if soaking cats in gasoline and setting them on fire is morally loathesome to the elders, it must be hilarious to the naughty boy, hilarious because he also knows how hideous it is. Or saying a dirty word; or pouring ink in the baptismal font. Or, as even the adult Benjamin Péret used to do in his dadaist moments, spitting on priests. Stealing a pear, with Augustine, missing classes with everybody, the vacation from duty.

Now all of these things from the hideous to the merely funny violate customary ethics; and yet in most cases, the particular violation is not a violation of anything ever explicitly spelled out. Custom, then, is not a list of things to do and things not to do; any such list would be infinite, and even then not serve the purpose of customary ethics. Customary ethics is more like a language, or a sense or style of life, codifiable only at key points, but nevertheless governing the sense of what may and may not be done, and what must be done. In my own case, my parents never told me explicitly that I was not to murder, lie, steal, cheat, or threaten them. These matters were all understood. Nor was that understanding based on the U.S. criminal code, which neither my parents nor I had ever read. I do not think I am exceptional in this respect. In short, everyone begins in an ethical world, the power and constitutive force of which is revealed as much in its ordinary obedience as in its infraction. Its force appears most strongly when it is violated. But obviously for the most part we do not violate it. We more or less breathe it as the assumed atmosphere in which we of course live. That it is so assumed is a good thing; but at the same time it tends to make itself invisible, somewhat like the invisible cosmos in which we also live.

Without custom, that is, attempting to live with either oneself or with others out of nothing but one's own desire and imagination or else reason itself, would not merely be a hopeless burden to put on oneself, resulting in such a freaky and personal style of life that one would be ejected from the society of one's fellows, but would render any society at all impossible. A few free spirits from time to time have tried it, such as Jacques Vaché, but they were and are all on the very fringe, if not beyond, anything that could resemble either the human world or possible members of it. Further, they are not in the least inventors of their own lives, but merely personal inverters of custom; and as every Hegelian knows, one does not free oneself from custom by negating it; merely reduplicating it in negative form logically and emotionally binds one to the negated enemy. Jacques Vaché committed suicide taking along with him two friends who were, no doubt at all, thus murdered.*

Our present point in all of this is the discovery of or encounter with the ethical, in the form of custom; its first appearance is that of an ancient and traditional, binding sense of good and evil, of what is demanded, allowed, and what impermissible and shameful. I discover this chiefly in any inclination I may have to violate it. Otherwise everything goes too smoothly for me to notice; I am usually good or at least inoffensive. But let me loose, and then I may discover, if I had not known it before in imagination, the frightful and over-

---

*The case of Jacques Vaché is interesting largely because it presents an impassioned attack on the moral as well as the poetic in the form of absolute indifference to value as such. It is documented in André Breton's *Les Pas Perdus* (Gallimard, 1969), pp. 15-22 and 59-63.

whelming force which customary ethics is prepared to exercise. That force is far more "objective" than the opposition of a brick wall. For in point of fact, my own life, already structured by ethics, finds that not merely are others prepared to compel obedience, but I am too, willy-nilly. Ethics, then, on this most foundational level is indeed constitutive of the sense of my life, and it manifests that power *any time I choose to disobey it*. It appears to me, growing up into human life, as there, external to my desires, originating from nowhere, or once upon a time, from the "establishment," or from God and the Founding Fathers — the interpretations may be what they are. The net result is the same: I encounter the constitutive rules of my life as already constituted, without my help or cooperation, and there with overwhelming power; their opposite is a moral chaos, that is, the disappearance of anything remotely resembling the human daylight world.

That men find themselves already within the ethical is hardly news; indeed, anyone who did not recognize the ethical would be regarded not so much as a new prophet as a moral idiot, and the rest would hardly have any choice but to imprison him away from those who did, as deficient in a natural capacity. Criminals, on the other hand, are understood to recognize the ethical but to have chosen to violate it. They must be punished, not to improve or rehabilitate them, nor to exact from them that which they denied their victim, but to restore the moral claim of the moral, which in this domain is ultimate. But our concern here is not with those who recognize the ethical and its ethical claim and violate it, but rather with the primordial recognition of the ethical itself.

It must go without saying that the ethical was never understood as simply what men have done in the past, that therefore the past as such is good. Anyone at all knows that the ethical custom which directs our sense of good and evil is not good and binding simply because it is past, or even that most men lived according to it. Indeed, it is also a common sentiment that no one ever lived ethically, that men of the past labored under as much self-criticism as those of the present, that the past was a past of terrible crime and sacrilege. Therefore, the good in custom is not in the least a statistical result of what men factually did, but rather an ideal, then as now. The sense of valorizing custom through the past reaches its true aim by projecting it to its extreme: the dream of the golden age or Garden of Eden, a "once upon a time" in which men did live in accordance with the ideal. Or a future millennial state, never to be historically reached, when men will once again rejoin their ideal. The past, then, which sanctifies custom does not have the sense of a historical past, which for the most part was unknown anyway to preliterate and non-historical societies, but a sense of origin. If custom is taken as the source and medium of the good, and custom is understood as how the ancestors acted or believed, the whole matter has little to do with what they factually said or did. Rather it is an effort to express an origin of what we now take to be good, namely, that its origin, whatever it is, is not in the least to be found with ourselves, but beyond in what is not ourselves, the ancestors, the past, more or less inscrutable.

The inscrutability of our moral origins and ethical customs means, of course, an inscrutability to our own common sense and reasoning. If indeed the holy commands and prohibitions were scrutable to us, we should have not the slightest need for the past; we should need only our own commonsensical reasoning, and armed with that and that alone, we should be blessedly free from the inscrutable burden of what appears as simply laid down, and therefore to our common understanding as arbitrary. But what appears and is arbitrary to the understanding is not therefore arbitrary *tout simplement*; to common understanding operating only with certain logical principles, it all could just as well have been otherwise. But to anyone living within an ethical culture, it could not have been otherwise, since it is constitutive of his ethical life, that is, himself, and no one can imagine himself concretely to be otherwise, another person, or the inhabitant of another wholly different culture. These wholly other persons, their customs, times, their gods, almost necessarily appear profane or simply incoherent variations on one's own life. Beyond lies nothing but an empty imagination, interesting in the arts and for entertainment, but abhorrent to act upon.

To the transcendental ego, indeed, moral choice appears arbitrary since that ego can of itself prefer neither life nor death; it eternally is. But to that same ego, committed (arbitrarily) to life, and not to any imagined life but to the concrete life within which it already finds itself, certain moral premises are already given. As moral custom, they are the fundamentally unjustifiable roots of morality, which serve as the roots of any further justification or argument. Since such grounds are grounds by choice of the ego or soul, and that transcendental ego is itself identical to God, those choices, assents, or absolute passions take on the form of the holy foundations of ethical life, at one and the same time an affirmation by the God within and therefore sacred, as well as inscrutable to the transcendental and intuitive reason within which the choice is founded, transcendentally free and morally binding upon itself.

Needless to say, these are reflections upon the dialectical grounds of the process and do not describe psychological events, deliberations, argumentations, or anything but an explication of an absolute situation within which, for the most part, we enact our lives in something of a stupor.

Within the scheme, however, one can place the infinite variety of attitudes toward the moral situation. The world pessimists, the world optimists, the courageous, the despondents, and that great massive range between, an attitude which is neither fanatically free, nor fanatically submerged, but takes each thing as it comes and makes its practical decision, accepting its defeats and enjoying its successes. Schopenhauer, Whitman, Raskolnikov obviously are not typifications of most men; they are transcendental attitudes toward transcendental choices. Those choices touch the sacred joy or sacred horror of life and what lies beyond. And so with the great founders of religion and culture. Without these foundational persons, their lives, deeds, and deaths, there would indeed be nothing but wandering, inconclusiveness, moral confusion, in a word, spiritual chaos and not spiritual world. And that is exactly where philosophical ethics finds its proper sphere of activity: interminable argumentation without foundation.

Rational philosophical critique is naturally very unhappy with anything inscrutable, fearing quite rightly that cloaking values with inscrutability is risky business indeed. Under that cloak the worst sins and vices might creep in, claiming equal sanction with virtue and the good. It seeks, therefore, to find a clear criterion, accessible to and defensible by that natural reason *anyone* can claim. Its first act is to discredit "mystery, miracle, and authority" (as Dostoievsky put it). This was not exclusively the work of the 18th century Enlightenment. It is inherent in the intention of reason or reflection itself. Its roots may even be seen in Plato and his hero, Socrates, who insisted on "following the argument, wherever it might lead." And yet Plato, who needless to say thought within a wholly different horizon from the shallows of the Enlightenment, never for an instant dreamed of inventing an ethics out of "pure reason" which can operate solely with the principle of non-contradiction. There was invariably a reference to piety, to the gods, and Socrates determined his response to the crises in his life by listening to his inner *daimon,* a procedure, however, he never seemed to have recommended to others. The Delphic Oracle gave him a special mission, not exactly universalizable to all men. Errors of thought could be exposed by thought or dialectic; but the positive substance was not exactly deducible from the principle of non-contradiction. In a word, there still remained within the supremely philosophical Plato a sense of reverence and awe before the transcendental form of the Good.

Not so, of course, with the Enlightenment thinkers and their present-day descendents, still searching for a formula of the good and its justification. Why be moral? Why be just? are asked, almost as though Plato's question in the *Republic* were being repeated — which verbally seems to be the case until one reads the actual inquiry.

But if it took Plato ten books of the *Republic* to explore the question, an exploration which finally involves a metaphysics, an epistemology, a psychology, a politics, an aesthetics, and virtually every other branch of philosophy, our modern friends dispose of it in an article. Not that we do not appreciate brevity, but the truncation in analysis of a complex of factors essentially bound together invariably begs the very question asked, providing nothing but a pseudo-solution. Perhaps the most typical of the analytic solutions is to point out that we ought to be good because that is what the term *good* means: that which we ought to pursue! The violation of duty thus turns out to be a violation of dictionary usage, a misuse of terms, and the criminal is one who has committed a semantic confusion! The great Kant, who was worlds removed from any such shenanigans, nevertheless also found the "unconditioned good"—that which was good under all possible circumstances—in a self-consistent will, a will which willed to be subservient to pure reason, a reason, moreover, which could have nothing before it but the universal concept. That Kant went far beyond this is not to our present point.

And then the Utilitarians, sensing the empty formalism of Kant's formulas, added "content"! The content was to be "happiness"; the good was now understood to be the greatest happiness of the greatest number, a formula which even begins to look scientific, since "greatest" is a quantitative term, and lent itself to computation in Bentham's "calculus of pleasures." This new formalism promised to be practical; it meant to resolve once and for all the endless disputes among philosophers either about what the good meant, or how it was to be achieved. Alas, for the Kantians, there seems no answer available as to why consistency or accordance with formal reason was itself good, without the presupposition that somehow reason is man's highest or most distinguishing faculty, all taken for granted by Kant; and alas for the Utilitarians, pleasures—being qualitative—do not in any sense appear to be additive; nor is it very obvious that pleasure, even its "greatest quantity," should appear to everyone as the good of life; nor is it obvious why I should prefer the greatest happiness of the greatest number to my own; in a word, we are back to where Plato began in the *Republic*: What is justice, and why should I be just?

The range of explanation for the ethical based upon what the common philosophical understanding can grasp as axiomatic is virtually endless. If one finds only self-interest plausible, another will oppose a natural benevolence found not only in some men but also in the animals; another will discover a faculty of value intuition, which simply sees that certain acts are evil, others good without further argument;

whereas yet another finds each such intuition itself most discussable in terms of the consequences of what it claims, everything being subject to discussion, experiment, and even votes.
Or indeed whether it was an intuition at all rather than a
rationalization of that which had its origin in either the id or
the hidden economic class-interests of the intuitor.

In all of these versions of the good or duty and their
philosophical comprehension, what we miss is anything that
could support the infinite passion that is poured into good
and evil themselves: the horror at unjustifiable killing, the
disgust with self-indulgence, the enthusiasm with which courage is greeted, and the transcendental joy of kindness and
charity. In short, the very substance of the good has been lost
and in its place a simulacrum presented — most usually, though
not always, under the aegis of *naturalism*. And, for the most
part, these abortive efforts to think the good rest upon an
effort to ground ethics on the nature of man, understood not
sacredly but profanely, whether that nature is analyzed into
natural passions such as egotism or benevolence or a mixture
of the two combined with fear and calculation, or a reason
not understood mystically or intuitively but rather as a faculty
for forming ideas and drawing their consistent conclusions or
for calculating, or finally the intuition of special essences of
value and their hierarchy, whose value oddly enough bears
little reference to him to whom they are to be of value. Now
it is not my intention to criticize philosophical reflections on
ethics on the grounds that the good or duty is defined through
and grounded upon man; anything else would be absurd. But
what bears criticism is the notion of man which has taken on
this foundational character. My own view is simply that nothing short of man — understood mystically as an identity of
himself and God — or a finite appearance of that which is

absolute could conceivably be adequate to the subject. And this is very far indeed from any naturalism or rationalism.

We must therefore raise a related question which I think must be addressed before ethical theory can be broached. It is not, Why be just or good? but rather, Why did men moralize themselves in the first place? By "moralizing themselves," I mean put themselves under the dominance of either the good or the just. What, then, is the origin of that mode of consciousness which not merely considers its own and others' acts under the category of the good, but which "must" do so? But the "must" now is a moral must, and not a naturalistic one of the form that heavy bodies must fall at the rate of $\frac{1}{2} gt^2$, nor a logical one of the form that a self-contradictory argument cannot be valid.

Why, then, did consciousness ever morally subject itself to the moral and the good? And more importantly, out of what resources, concealed perhaps within itself, did it do so? The phrasing "moralizing itself," applied to consciousness, is designed to call attention again to the fact that the transcendental ego is transcendentally free to act as it wills; it is, as Descartes shows, absolutely free, and in this respect shares the absolute freedom of God. For Descartes, our will is as free as the will of God, although obviously the range of its possible effectivity is limited to its body and the world interpreted by it. It is therefore a situated absolute. And so there always remains within the transcendental ego the possibility of affirming or consenting to its effectivity or life in the world, or withholding it altogether. Of course, these are extreme boundaries, but nevertheless that infinite freedom of the transcendental ego can never be wholly ignored; there are indeed occasions when it is exercised, as in absolute Zen withdrawal — absolute indifference to the choice of either life or death — or in suicide, or cases of final pathological withdrawal, and pessimism. The final consent to die by the dying, the acceptance and final embrace of death as a blessed release not merely from the vital agonies of the terminal illness but, in cases, from the burden of living at all, bear witness to these final resources of the spirit. The spirit at last may most keenly aspire to be by itself.

It would, I think, be a bad mistake to think of these ultimate choices as within the compass of ethical theory. The choice is not of a higher good, but of abandoning the horizon of good and evil altogether, into the "peace which passeth all understanding." Such final acts could hardly be justified as "contributing to the greatest happiness of the greatest number" without a profound falsification of their meaning to those making the choice. As an irrevocable and final choice, it can hardly even be comprehended on the probability scale of whether or not it contributes to greater happiness; and if the avoidance of pain might for a moment seem most acceptable in certain cases of agonizing terminal illness, in other more radical cases, it more clearly seems equally an avoidance of any further pleasure, a reversion to a mode of being where there is no longer either pleasure or pain in any sense in which those terms bear any analogy to their living counterparts.

This intentionality of the ego finally to withdraw from both the pains and pleasures of life, a philosophical suicide, has at least the merit and interest of suggesting the absolute transcendence of the ego in its function of will. It is indeed transcendent in principle and in actuality to its own bodily life; it considers whether it will or will not consent further to whatever life has to offer. It was not regarded by Kant as morally defensible; it was exactly an escape from the moral domain, and for him, morality can hardly permit anything to escape its judgment.

And yet these extreme cases of going "beyond good and

evil," while they illustrate a mystical indifference to the values of life, do not of themselves do much to clarify the domain of the moral itself. Why, then, did the transcendental ego, in and of itself, out of its own eternal and inherent freedom, choose to place itself under the category of duty or the good, in a word, the moral? And out of what resources within itself, since it must have such resources if the whole project is to be its act and make any sense to it? Some basic responses have been alluded to: the subjection of its will to reason, to maximize happiness, or because that's what the word *moral* means. Or indeed because our ancestors were moral, and their answer, lost in the beginnings of time, has become our law and custom. Or because God wills it, or, or, or . . . and the list trails off into the indefinite. However, all of these answers seem but dodges away from certain inescapable phenomenological facts. If morality is a derivate of natural law, the law of the sub-human, what moral reason could we have for taking it seriously? If the natural law is the law governing the sub-human, we surely have no obligation to hold ourselves down to that, and most moral theories are perfectly prepared to defend a human morality which transcends nature, now appearing as the "law of the jungle." And if it is the law of our nature, how is our nature being conceived? As a rational animal? But this cannot mean that we always are rational, but merely that we have a faculty for being so, a faculty lamentably infrequently exercised. And how is it exercised? If in logic or the sciences, either speculative or applied, then what could possibly follow pertinent to human choice? If "practical reason" with Kant, then it is indeed difficult to see what obligation the free will should have to rationalize itself, universalize its motivation, and derive therefrom some fixed duties which, spelled out in Kant, seem far more questionable than the feeling of the "human heart" from which Kant takes his start. And as for the now indefinite number of utilitarianisms, they owe their plausibility mostly to an inveterate habit of naturalists of finding ultimate philosophical satisfaction in any answer which traces the specifically human back to the frankly animal: desires for pleasure, instincts which may be found in analogous form among other mammals, etc. Reason, then, appears as foresight in providing more of these for me, avoiding pains for me; any fellows are dragged in either by another instinct, sympathy, or empathy, or as providing me with a safer and more secure scene where my own pleasures may be pursued.

Now all of these appear to us as dodges out of the very center of the problem. And I believe there is only a single answer which directly addresses the problem of morality. That answer places the sacredness or dignity of the person as both the origin and end of morality. The sacredness and dignity of the person are not postulates as with Kantian theory, but nothing more nor less than the rational-mystical intuition we have been discussing all along: that the transcendental ego itself is identical with the consciousness of God of Himself, in a word, that man is God, or more accurately, God in a living situation, but God nonetheless. And it is this intuition, remaining implicit or asleep but nonetheless felt, which animates the ethical consciousness. If frequently thought of as a feeling, a matter of the heart, a piety, a respect for the final value of each person, the intuition that it is indeed so only clearly confirms what the heart or conscience felt, a sentiment that with the human person, wherever it can be recognized, the sacred has become alive among us and, morally speaking, cannot be ignored. It can in fact be ignored, since the transcendental ego cannot forego its transcendental freedom; it can ignore the whole business, or can indeed choose to flout the moral and gratuitously choose defilement; but if it moralizes itself, then that act is to choose to recognize the sacredness of the person, the violation of which dialectically carries with it guilt, self-condemnation, and shame.

The intentionality which is the origin of morality, then, is nothing other than the choice to worship God, not in his absolute being as such, but as manifest most explicitly in the living human person wherever that can be recognized. It is therefore the choice of the Holy to love itself — none of which is intended to exclude a recognition of the presence of the absolute in various degrees in defective persons or, finally, in animals, where with the smallest amount of sympathy one can find instinctively or naturally the same presence, but charmingly asleep, or only vaguely awake. Still, the human face is not the animal snout, and the eyes are the windows of the awake soul.

B. The Beautiful

> Why do we weep on seeing the beautiful unless it offered
> us a foretaste of the glories beyond the grave?
> After: Edgar Allen Poe,
The Poetic Principle

The present discussion would be even more incomplete than it is if it were taken to be an aesthetics, a theory of the arts, or anything but a limited examination of the presuppositions of one distinctive domain of experience, that of the beautiful. Like the good, the beautiful has surrounding it the odor of the obsolete, stagnant, rotten, in any case, something so old-fashioned that none of us today could possibly take an interest in it. Do any of the arts now aim at anything that could possibly be called beautiful? Or rather do we now not demand the interesting, the shocking, the absurd, the self-expressive, the socially significant, at all costs the advanced without limit?

Les Beaux Arts, do they not belong to the academy of the 18th and 19th centuries in their least attractive and most pedantic sides? Meanwhile, as for the arts, it has now reached the point where anything whatsoever could properly be included under the term if a sufficient number of critics, curators, and gallery owners decided it was henceforth to be art.* And how are these poor souls to decide except through personal tastes, whim, profitability, the temper of the times, with more than one anxious eye on what their colleagues are up to?

Our own subject, then, shall not be "art" but rather the beautiful in either art or nature. Hence, if there ever was anything beautiful or perceived as beautiful, we will have more than enough to discuss. What makes the beautiful beautiful, and why should we take any interest in it? "Interest," however "disinterested" as with Kant, is hardly the right idea. The truth is that the greatest artists took their art with the very greatest of seriousness bordering on that holy terror appropriate to a ceremony for God Himself. Indeed, can one have an "interest" in such matters? And if the serious artist worked under a dedication, so did his appropriate fellow celebrants. Both worked or saw and heard in reverence: God — or the absolute — might appear; is one "interested' in an evoc-

*George Dickie has defended this approach in his *Art and the Aesthetic: An Institutional Analysis* (Cornell University Press, 1974) *passim*.
But the United States Customs Office has anticipated Mr. Dickie by regulations some seventy years old. When I recently brought back some masks and figures from New Guinea, they were declared to be "artifacts" rather than works of art, and thus subject to duty. The criteria used had some amusement value: to be judged as art, the work had to have been exhibited three times, it must be signed by the artist (in the present case, the "artists" were all illiterate), "native" works were not allowed and "native" was understood to be those who wore few if any clothes, and so on through an increasingly comical list of criteria. It was evident that these criteria were almost designed to save the customs inspector from having to make an aesthetic judgment, not such a bad idea after all.

ation of the holy? All of which is a far cry from expecting the artist's self to appear, or from worshipping the rules of the game, its presiding critics, let alone hoping for bitter social comment disguised as a drama, poem, picture, or building. And this sacred honor is still visible; a hush comes over the audience, the curtain rises, the conductor raises his baton; the image is surrounded by a frame, and silence is preserved in the gallery. When these do not prevail and are deliberately avoided, it is defiantly to fight them for a new "liberation," and not to ignore them altogether. Reverence in that case is still present if only by its denial.

"Beautiful" is itself only an approximate term to name our subject matter. It is difficult to imagine Aeschylus' or Sophocles' or Shakespeare's audiences forming the judgment "This is beautiful" after the performance. Not that these works were ugly or ill-made, but the word *beautiful* could not express anything remotely like the power of the work itself. Nor would it be likely that anyone, after a military funeral or the Mass, would be moved to pronounce it "beautiful." For Aristotle, the purpose of tragedy is to effect catharsis or purification, and for others a "reconciliation of man with the gods," or with himself, or with justice and necessity. Something therefore far more metaphysical or, if I may so put it, mystical, is involved in the great arts than the "beautiful" — which too easily lends itself to a slippage into the "pretty," the "aesthetic," or what Hegel disdainfully called "the art of the confectioner." The great arts, then, are far more analogous to religious rituals than to gallery displays or entertainment. And so, the proper word is lacking, but the thing we are looking for is not. In any event, the "aesthetic" increasingly looks like a specification of the beautiful, invented perhaps in the 19th century and lasting into ours and maybe already on its way out, having served its purpose.

In all this swamp of ambiguity — an ambiguity which could easily be repeated for religion, politics, and philosophy itself, each of which names a cluster of radically distinct things which must be historically and phenomenologically clarified — a few things about the beautiful might be isolated for discussion. Whatever the beautiful is, it does not offer itself to just any attitude of mind. One is not always ready for the beautiful, and one can easily lose it in the business of life, the need for action, the pressures of desire. And so the first moment of our discussion will be to repeat a few things which anyone can easily confirm for himself about that posture or attitude of the spirit to which the beautiful can appear, what is frequently called the aesthetic attitude or, with Kant, the "judgement of taste." The second moment will turn to the objective side, namely, that phenomenal objectivity which the aesthetic attitude apprehends, the beautiful object. They are, of course, in strict correlation. But then, this is only a start in isolating the phenomenon I wish to discuss. The end will be to show how the entire phenomenon would be impossible for anything but a transcendental ego implicitly identical with the absolute; in other words, the domain of the beautiful is another example of the mystical grounds of genuinely human life; hence its seriousness and significance. The "aesthetic attitude" can be seen, then, either as profanation or consecration of the sacred.

1. The aesthetic attitude. Under the title "judgment of taste," Kant characterizes the aesthetic attitude through four "moments," one of which is "disinterested interest"; Edward Bullough characterizes it through "aesthetic distance"; Croce as "expressive intuition"; Eliseo Vivas as "rapt intransitive attention." For all the differences, it is perfectly clear that the experience of the beautiful bears marked differences from what may be called ordinary experience. Cézanne's apples are not experienced through hunger, nor the Apollos and Aphrodites of Greek sculpture experienced through lust. Not, of course, that these interests of ordinary experience are lacking, but then they have been transmuted by the aesthetic attitude into something else, something disinterested, too, intuitive, and intransitive. The direct interests and desires are *aufgehoben* from their instinctive desire to consume and possess into what is content to look with rapt attention. And with music, the sounds in their structures are heard, and not taken simply as signals of fright, terror, warnings, or the love cries of the amorous. And so with disinterested interest, the interest is hardly blotted out, leaving us with something wholly indifferent to our desires but, while there, is also not the final word. The aesthetic attitude, then, achieves a paradoxical or dialectical mood: while attending to the phenomena of the world, and attending to them as they relate to our human being, at the same time it does not react to those phenomena as consciousness ordinarily would: it is content to look, to see, and to hear for the first time what the phenomena are. It is dominated by intuition, an immediate seeing, and not by the existential agitations simply of concern, care, or desire. All of this is somewhat cliché in aesthetics, and anyone can confirm their justice by himself. Without a certain participation in the direct sense of what is offered, aspects of the world, the subject matter would sink immediately into the senseless; a man would no longer be a man, a mountain no longer a mountain, and Cézanne's apples no longer apples. For their meaning as human beings, mountains, and apples, we must at some level encounter these phenomena as we do in ordinary life, and yet that encounter is not aesthetic. The aesthetic, while preserving the significance of the things of the world, at the same time reduces itself to looking at them, listening to them for what they are. No wonder, then, that philosophers as diverse as Schelling, Hegel, and Croce found in aesthetic intuition a primary source of our acquaintance with being. If "knowledge" means a discursive, problematic, and basically useful acquaintance with the world, intuition is not knowledge; but if knowledge also implies the fundamental source of our awareness of what is, then intuition is knowledge *par excellence*. Husserl's phenomenology itself was nothing less than a persistent effort to return "back to the things themselves" as they offered themselves to our own living awareness, stripped bare of our hypotheses, no matter of what sort they were. And for Hegel, art was the immediacy in imagination of the *absolute spirit* itself, absolute because on a different plane than either subjective spirit with its finite desires, or merely objective spirit living within the historical institutions of the state. All these modes of spirit were raised into the absolute spirit which was no longer perspectival, did not look at the world exclusively through the eyes of appetite nor political distress or success, but at last looked at its world without wishing in that mood so much to change it as see it as it is.

But then our present question concerns the foundations of such experience, namely, what sort of mind renders such a paradoxical miracle possible? If human being or the ego were strictly and exclusively "surrendered over to the world," as Heidegger has it, or *"engagé"* with Sartre, then indeed the aesthetic experience would be impossible. For obviously the aesthetic attitude, while contemplating its world, is not in the least surrendered over to it, nor engaged in its temptations and dreads. It prefers to look at and listen to that world. And so it immediately follows that the ego enacting aesthetic experience is of such a sort that it can also be detached while attached, and what is detachment in this connection but precisely that transcendental feature we have been studying from the outset? In a word, the ego can only assume the aesthetic attitude if it is transcendental to its own vital association with its finite life. The aesthetic attitude, then, confirms the transcendental nature of the ego and is an exercise of it. And to remark with Hegel that it is a form of absolute spirit only says again that the transcendental ego is indeed the consciousness of absolute reality, imaginatively concrete in the present case; it sees itself and others as we live in, rule over, and dominate our own vital life. Is it that much unlike mystical rapture? Or the strange peace which descends in religious or philosophical understanding? Schopenhauer in the penultimate chapter of *The World as Will and Idea* found salvation in it, just short of the total extinction of the will. A catharsis for Aristotle, and on the ladder of love, for Plato a possible vision of an ultimate form of beauty, not remote from either the good or *the one.*

2. *The aesthetic object.* If the aesthetic *attitude* is a mood or act of the transcendental ego, that is to say, absolute spirit, what must be said about its favorite *object,* the beautiful? In the history of the arts, we can see a progressive democratization of candidates for the title. At the beginning, only stories, myths, and tales of gods and heroic men. And then the gods dropped out, or became themselves humanized; and finally the men need no longer be heroic at all; nature itself was admitted, home life, still lives, popular dance tunes, and now perhaps it can be said, absolutely anything. All of this has, of course, its own account and logic, but then that account in its willingness to see absolutely anything as an appropriate object of the aesthetic attitude is not so much to our purpose, as another account which looks for the most appropriate object for the aesthetic attitude, namely, the beautiful, whether in art or nature.

But if the aesthetic attitude is that which wants to see or intuit, the question answers itself; intuition doesn't wish to go anywhere else; it prefers to dwell with its object. It is, as Vivas says, "intransitive." Now then, what is intuitable? If intuition wishes to see, what is indeed visible? What can be listened to? A half-sentence, so understood, offers intuition only a half-intuition; in and of itself it demands completion by what is not presented, and therefore disturbs intuition, makes a demand upon it which it itself does not satisfy. Intuition can only rest in the intuitable. Hence, since intuition looks for what it can grasp, its favorite object must always be a whole, a whole presented to it. Parts, fragments, hints, ruins, bits, and portions may indeed be more exciting to the imagination, since they demand, in and of themselves, to be filled out in order for them to be themselves. But we are not exactly looking at this point for the exciting, but rather that rest in rapture which is achieved in the beautiful. Put otherwise, the ego can only have a vision of the visible, and not everything as it first offers itself is visible; more likely it hints at something else, anticipates or adumbrates something else, is transitive just as real things in the real world are.

But then, aesthetic experience is not ordinary experience, engaged in fighting for the delights and life of its vitality. It is content to look. And so if ordinary things as ordinarily experienced clearly and necessarily whirl us into a vortex of finite things, no one of which can be itself without an indefinite circumambient world, the aesthetic experience lifts us and its object out of that vortex of relativities, to dwell with something that at last is itself phenomenally, is a sort of whole, indeed a sort of absolute. Each work of art, then, offers intuition a version of the whole, a world, an absolute beyond which the ego is not urged to move.

Each work of art, insofar as it aspires to the beautiful, presents intuition with a whole, a world, a unity, which makes no significant demand for anything else. And insofar as ordinary experience rarely offers such perfect wholes, or absolutes, imagination is called upon to forge what can rarely be encountered in life. That life and nature do offer such found beauties is undeniable, sometimes in the lower orders: perfect crystals, perfect flowers, and perfect animals, all miraculously beautiful, and looking as though they were made specifically for aesthetic intuition. But when the subject matter rises to the human level, the difficulty mounts: if we look for perfect actions, actions which are historically or in fact carried through in their dialectical sense, history or the chronicle has to be helped out a little with fiction, and the dreaming imagination has more than a little work to do.

And if this is one function of the imagination, another is to raise the record of the factual existent to the level of inexistence by representation. If intuition desires to rest in its vision and not ultimately be troubled by the seductive or menacing, how better assuage it than by offering it what it already knows to be images, performances, representations? Then it need not be disturbed by murder on the stage or only read about. Nor need it be tempted to climb Cézanne's *Mont Ste-Victoire*.

Anything which offers itself to the imagination as a whole can easily be said to offer an objectification of the absolute, since wholeness is, ontologically speaking, the essential nature of the absolute itself. Granted, these are but aspects or particularizations of the absolute, nevertheless they do have the predicate "whole" if they are beautiful, and further they offer their phenomenal selves in an imaginative medium to intuition. Aesthetic intuition then sees what some argument might try to prove, that there is *wholeness*, even if in some particular form.*

3. *Fracture once again healed.* Our brief excursion into romantic philosophical aesthetics has shown, it is hoped, that the aesthetic intuition of the beautiful has nothing whatever in common with ordinary practical experience; it is indeed a vision of some concrete aspect of the absolute, possible only to an ego which is transcendental and itself, even in a dreaming mood, the absolute identity of ego and absolute. It can hardly be a mystery, then, why serious artists and serious audiences take serious art seriously. More is involved and more at stake than self-expression, social commentary, pleasure, or excitement. Hanging before one's eyes and passing through one's ears is the absolute itself, the sacred and not the profane; and its proper fruit is not so much pleasure as spiritual joy; is it not a celebration of the divine rather than man, except insofar as they are seen as the same?

C. Truth

The transcendental ego is itself the subjectivity of absolute reality first taken as absolute object, but in which both itself and that absolute reality are apprehended as one. It is therefore in its essence, the essential intuition of God by God. This intuition itself constituting the ego may be explicit as in the perfection of mystic experience, or implicit, down through any number of grades of consciousness until it seems almost lost in objective perception, desires, volitions, actions, and even objectifying reflections upon itself. Nonetheless, even the most biological or animal activities of the ego exhibit its sleeping presence even when forgotten or explicitly denied. Human life

*Cf. my *Public Sorrows and Private Pleasures* (Indiana University Press, 1976), chap. 7, "Art as Philosophy," for a development of this theme.

is distinguished from animal life in all its phases; even the most retarded, undeveloped, or psychotically distorted human consciousness is still human consciousness. It does not seem possible for it to become strictly animal. Even the most distorted human consciousness or life is not that of the normal animal but rather of a very abnormal animal indeed.

In any event, the transcendental ego itself is inherently the truth of God considered as absolute reality. It is ineluctably in the ontological position of being true, so long as it is the meditation upon or intuition of God. And for this, it has no need of method or additional confirmation, both of which would constitute absurdities. What indeed would guarantee them? Hence the essentiality and in principle certainty of both the Cartesian *cogito* and the ontological argument. It is, of course, a matter of principle, a realizable ideal; not everything that passes through the mind, nor any chance attitude of a wavering consciousness need be an intuitive truth. But the only thing which can certify metaphysical intuition is that intuition itself, and such accompanying reflections as might remove its false surrogates, which is the basic task of this book. But seeing is indeed seeing, and nothing can change that. Not everything can be intuited, and discursive argument can help to remove from claims to intuition the unintuitable; the domain of what it is possible to intuit is limited. For example, it is certainly not possible to intuit any contingent fact. Or, as Santayana put it succinctly, "nothing *given* exists"; existence attributes to what is given another ontological status, to wit, that it is externally related to and dependent upon something else not given, to an indefinite field of other existents or the world. To intuit or to be given something therefore removes that given from the domain of contingent existence; as phenomenon or given, it is what it is, but it cannot have, as given or phenomenon, the predicate of existence. This is, obviously, no objection to the intuition of God or absolute reality, since God is not an existent, contingently or externally related to what He is not, but eternal being as absolute. George Fox, then, was certainly confused when he affected to see in certain states of mind the medical properties of herbs in the field, something we can know to be not an affair of intuition at all.

That the transcendental ego is itself the intuition of absolute reality, the extraordinary claim of the rational mystics, might seem to suffer from the very obvious fact, that only rational mystics or metaphysicians seem to affirm it. But then this is a trivial objection; our daily vital interests and concerns focus on the finite, the existential, that which can be sought or avoided; and neither the ego nor its absolute reality belongs to that category. Invisible like a dramatist, they may preside over the whole affair, but are not members of the cast. Nothing in human life would be the same if they were not; and yet their dominance over that life is itself transcendental. There could not be, we have argued, either the good, the beautiful, and now truth unless these were themselves various modalities of the transcendental ego, in its absolute solidarity with God. The misinterpretation of the transcendental into events, things, mental states, or the sensorily perceptible is, of course, nothing less than superstition. And while nothing happens for us or can have meaning for us without it, it is not itself an event or happening. Not all causes or essential factors in happenings and life need themselves be happenings or vital events, an ancient truth sometimes forgotten.

The fundamental source of all truth of whatever sort is the immediate relation, through seeing, of transcendental subjectivity and its object when that object is indeed intuitable. Clearly the only object which can, in and of itself, be seen in intuition, is that which in and of itself is a whole or absolute.

A part or phase of something else cannot in and of itself,
according to its own meaning of being a part, be seen; it
demands its whole which makes it what it is. And since there
can be *only one absolute,* the absolute is the sole intuitable
object. The intuition of God, therefore, is the ontological foundation of the ego, as well as the epistemological foundation
of any other intuition, proposition, or argument which might
seek to adumbrate it. The essence of the ego is to be the truth
of God.

Now, some infrequently noticed conclusions follow almost immediately, severely delimiting the range of application
of formal logic, the perpetual enemy of mystical reason. But
does formal logic have a delimited range? Can it indeed account for its own claims to universal validity, and then serve
as the final critic of mystical claims? Or does formal logic
itself need to undergo a transcendental critique preserving its
usefulness yet assigning it to only certain ontological domains? Our contention is that, no matter how formal it pre-
tends to be, it always is limited by its implicit, finite content
or reference.

First, we must recall certain things said about the essence
of absolute reality and its transcendental ego.

Absolute reality, or perfect (completed) reality, is by essence and definition transcendental to any of its modes. And
so, mystically it is neither exclusively here nor there, now nor
then. Or, conversely, it is everywhere and always, since each
where and when is but a mode of it. In itself, therefore, it is
a coincidence of opposites, and if the two previous examples
are drawn from space and time, the list could be extended *ad
infinitum.* Formal logic, on the other hand, must find any
such notion as absolute reality pure nonsense. The foundations of formal logic include the identity of each thing with
itself, the impossibility of contradictory predicates applying

to the same subject (at the same time and in the same respect, although Kant himself rejects this Aristotelian qualification), and that there is no middle between contradictory predicates, or propositions. Bishop Butler's famous "each thing is what it is and not another thing" sums it up briefly. We shall not be concerned here with the dispute as to whether the three "laws of thought" are or are not reducible to one. It makes no difference for our purposes. But what does make a difference is that none of these laws of logical thought, held to be the presuppositions of either all meaning or all valid thought, can be justified for the entire range of thought. If they are the defining principles of formal logic, the sole conclusion is that formal logic is not formal enough, and conceals right in its defining criteria a limitation; it may be formal in certain regards, but right from the start it bears an implicit reference to possible finite objects. Assuming that that is all there is, formal logic can move on as swiftly as it likes, and never encounter a finite opposed case. But then our question concerns the infinite; to that, these so-called laws of thought cannot apply. Formal logic, then, feels itself upon safe ground in concluding that the absolute is senseless, "babbling," as Aristotle has it, and with babbling, the philosopher need have nothing to do. And of course, if the subject were finite in character, then indeed one would babble in violating the conditions of discourse about the finite. But since the subject matter, on the face of it, is not finite, then indeed one is babbling about it when one blithely applies the principles of formal, i.e., finite logic. That absolute reality is infinite follows from its essential meaning. That such a meaning also is, and is necessarily, is the burden of the ontological argument, or intuition, as it is treated here. Hence there is such a reality, and formal logic is incapable of concerning itself with it, and under no circumstances may be permitted to work as a criterion or canon for anything predicated of absolute reality. For formal logic, absolute reality must remain outside its proper area of surveillance, perhaps — at its most generous — an outside possibility. But if for formal logic God at least falls into *terra incognita*, for the rational mystic that *terra* is no longer *incognita*, but cognized in metaphysical or rational intuition.

And, of course, the same applies *mutatis mutandi* to the transcendental ego, which after all is the intuition of both itself and absolute reality. The ego which intuits absolute reality — and coevally itself, through subjective participation — is most obviously nothing whatsoever that could even remotely be called finite. It surely is related to finite perceptions, volitions, and in general most immediately to its own living body, none of which is possible without it. What then is it that makes the affirmations and denials considered under formal logic but precisely the transcendental ego itself, now turning its attention to these assertions, denials and entailments? What is it that in making any affirmation, makes it against a corresponding denial? For every affirmed yes, there is a rejected no; otherwise there would be no affirmation whatsoever, but a mere state of mind. And, even when the ego affirms its own formal principles for their finite work, it must have in mind what it is denying. And so indeed there must be that which in its logical imagination can entertain the contradictory, even if only to reject it. This infinite power of the ego to entertain the contradictory precisely in its rejection of one side is most remarkable; for the contradictory is nothing but another name for the *infinite absolute*, the contradictory enclosing the universe of discourse. And so, in the end, the transcendental ego which developed its own formal logic, itself falls outside it, and would have to do so if it is the origin of even that logic. Thus, this particular product of the ego, useful as it may be for its own purposes, is incapable of comprehending that very transcendental ego which generated it. Does the son indeed ever know his father?

And so our conclusion can only be that neither absolute reality or God, nor the transcendental ego in and of itself, can possibly be embraced by formal logic, or any formal ontology whose foundational principle rests upon such laws of logic.

Our quarrel, then, is not with any legitimate application of formal logic, but its pretention to operate as a criterion of either truth or meaning in a domain closed to it by its own first principles.

The joy of the contradictory, the *coincidentia opposito-rium* which is the very life of the transcendental ego or self, and God Himself, puts to shame the finite precisions of formal logic, and indeed opens the soul up to itself. If truth, then, has so long passed for correctness of either judgment or propositions about some finite state of affairs, and therefore passed into the domain of the essentially trivial, practical, and boring, the magnificent lesson of mystical reason tells us something altogether different, not subject to those foolish laws of thought which are only laws of very finite thought, but something which announces a perpetual return to what altogether lies beyond law itself, namely the internal, intrinsic, and essential life of the self. Formal logic, in these terms, is simply blasphemous when ignorant of its own limits.

Truth, of course, in virtually any primordial sense of the term, has nothing whatsoever to do with these trivialities. Truth as a moral value is certainly not a correctness of statement about something lying outside. In English, the term is related to *troth*, which is the same as loyalty or faith. When true, I am faithful to friends and the God in them and in me. Therefore, the contrary to truth is not incorrectness, but betrayal; how indeed is it possible to betray objective states of affairs, such as "the cat is on the mat or not"? It would only be the most far-fetched analogy which could stretch the term to such lengths that it had lost virtually every vestige of its essential and primordial sense. The passion for truth which men of good will manifest is certainly not a matter of ascertaining the exact chemical composition of water or the number of grains of sand on the beach. It always was and remains a passion for recognizing and honoring the divinity in oneself and the other. And so, good-bye to formal logic for this domain; it not merely has nothing to say but lives in a perpetual offense to what everyone always and already knew anyway, the mystical origin and meaning of truth.

Appendixes

The following appendixes are offered as supplemental to the main text. The first, *Mysticism and Drugs*, looks into the genuineness of drugged mysticism, but also its dialectical deterioration. In the second and third appendixes, two versions of the ontological argument turn it all over again; why repeat the argument? For any justification, I must revert to what is one of the constant themes of the main text: the central aim of this small book is mystical reason, and its purpose is to be of aid in comprehension. Comprehension can be assisted in a number of ways, but here it consists in turning over and over again the very core of the subject; hence it may be of some help in dwelling upon what is essentially the same thing, from a number of angles, a number of moods, and perhaps a number of phrases which on the level of argument may seem to be sheer repetition. If the whole effort of philosophy is to comprehend ultimate matters, that comprehension may be more assisted by revolving an infinite subject matter about our own small perspectives, than by multiplying arguments *ad infinitum*; hence my apology for the repetition.

The fifth appendix will be of interest only to those who have read some previous works of mine, *Objectivity*, *The Autobiographical Consciousness*, and *Public Sorrows and Private Pleasures*.* Perhaps to a casual reading, these works as a whole may seem to be incoherent, and their author distracted indeed. Maybe these brief remarks will help to put all these works, including the present one, in whatever order they have, and do something toward removing the suspicion of incoherence.

*William Earle, *Objectivity: An Essay in Phenomenological Ontology* (New York: Times Books, 1968); *The Autobiographical Consciousness* (New York: Times Books, 1972); *Public Sorrows and Private Pleasures* (Bloomington: Indiana University Press, 1976).

Appendix I Mysticism and Drugs

The ego, as we have seen, has two functions, or — put otherwise — can be taken in two respects. In and by itself, it is
transcendental to existence, that is, an eternal actuality which
cannot be essentially characterized by any existential predicate: it is not a process, an event, a sequence of motions, not
material or spatial in any sense; in a word, it is absolute. Its
being is characterized by eternity, actuality, and self-identity,
and whatever other transcendental predicates can be derived.
It is not born, cannot die, yet eternally is. This it knows by
self-intuition and is certain, not inferential or hypothetical.
On the other hand, it also finds itself alive and existing. It is
the ego of a person who is born, will die, and whose life is
his existence with others in a temporal and material world.
The ego, then, has two aspects or functions; by itself and
with existence. If these two functions and their appropriate
domains are ontologically distinguishable, so are the functions of the ego. And if they are distinguishable, there is the
possibility of their dissociation. By dissociation, I here mean
only that the transcendental ego may but need not associate
itself with that existence which proceeds from its own living
body. But even so, *associate* is not the appropriate term: the
association of the ego with the life of its own body is hardly
an association, if that term is understood as accompanying
that life. Rather it animates that life, adopts it, forms and
controls it, and attempts to penetrate it with its own intrinsic
being. In short, it gives to and receives from that existence
meaning. It interprets, remembers, anticipates, and comprehends existence to whatever extent it can; it lives with others
who become important to it; it reflects upon its existence; and
ultimately tries to come to terms with both the origin and
cessation of its existence. This it does in its own terms and

for itself. It is how the transcendental ego is with the life it consents to live. This life is not necessarily bound to that of the ego; it may be profoundly rejected, vacated, and even found repulsive. After all is said, there is always an ontological heterogeneity between the timeless and the existential flux of existence. There is also always an amenability of existence to the transcendental purposes of the ego. For Plato, who was largely concerned with the radical difference between the senses and reason, there was also that third "organ," the heart, which could serve as mediator, or, as in the *Republic*, between the philosophical rulers and the economic workers, the soldiers, who could listen to reason, and practically carry out in life what they heard. The chaos of the state occurs when the soldiers no longer listen but act on their own, taking over the highest governing function. The state is the soul writ large, and so in the soul there must be discerned a mediating function between the transcendental and the living senses. This function is directed toward the ordering and comprehension of life, but does so through and for the ego. Whether "will" or "heart," it represents the ego's transcendental affirmation to penetrate existence with itself. Thus, one may or may not have the "heart to live," or — following Tillich — the "courage to be." Now of course, the ego is in no necessity of doing so; it may indeed withdraw its fundamental consent to or affirmation of existence in order to be by itself, with its own appropriate eternal world. Such is something like the abrupt mystic's choice, those who leave the world, do not return, and in effect sunder their bond with life. Nothing in it is essential to them anymore, and they live on in complete indifference to that life. But such is also the point where a certain phenomenological sense of drugged experience becomes intelligible.

Since this mediating function between the transcendental

ego and life, has, so to speak, one foot in each, perhaps it is
not surprising that its own activity will be affected by agencies which are definitely existential, to wit, drugs, as well as
natural agencies such as hormonal imbalances, none of which
can be accurately said to cause any transcendental phenomena, but rather should be said to facilitate, release, or even
induce them. And what indeed do they induce except that
radical dissociation of the transcendental from the existential
characterized by abrupt mysticism and the far stages of drug
addiction?

What, then, are some typical phenomena in drugged experience? Here the transcendental ego reverts to its own realm,
and what it says is remarkably like what some mystics say:
"I am GOD!" Now to ascribe this solely to a particular form
of physiological euphoria misses the phenomenological point.
The sole phenomenological point is the explication of this
meaning as it is in and for the ego meaning it. But we have
already presented sufficient evidence from a variety of perspectives, that the ego in its transcendental role is indeed
absolute, precisely as it affirms. That a more circumspect
reflection might for certain purposes also wish to make distinctions, is nothing to our present point — which is the sense
of the experience to the experiencer, and its unshakeable core
of truth. No one could possibly have the experience expressed
in "I am God," if the self having such experience were nothing
but an epiphenomenon of physiological processes, no matter
how understood. Once released from its existential concerns,
the ego, relieved from a burden, now is in its own proper
domain, the eternal, the one, the absolute, to wit itself as it
is for itself transcendentally.

In its first stage, it may try to drag along with it those
functions of itself which are most amenable to absolute freedom; the preference of the addict for music, mathematics, and

poetry is notorious. The aversion to the practical, the political, the long-range project equally notorious. The imagination, freed from any practical purpose, luxuriates in itself trying to follow and express the absolute through paradox. The "exotic" expresses the strangeness of its new life to the former world. For the Westerner, that exotic is the East, its figurations, mythologies, languages, in which their exotic character is essential. But even for the East, their character remains exotic to the practical world, though obviously not culturally. The graphic style is characteristic: a marked preference for the arabesque, the curvilinear form, the intertwined, with an equally marked aversion to the straight line, the square, or anything too representational; the straight line is the old, rational, practical will which has been abandoned, and representational pictures are too redolent of the world now abandoned. Further, the intertwining expresses the mutual interdependence of all finite beings, each in itself nothing but a false abstraction from an infinite living whole. All these expressions, whether from Northwestern America, Indochina, New Guinea, the drawings of schizophrenics in hospitals, or the advertising art of Madison Avenue, bear a marked family resemblance. The Islamic arabesque itself, developed under a religion with proscriptions against carving graven images of creation but, as Hegel put it, in their infinite multiplicity and variation, trying vainly to exhaust the absolute, is the classical archetype. If it finds its way elsewhere, even among the Indians of the Northwest Coast, it is hardly surprising that at least what we call the "arts," were there "holy," "sacred," and for the most part done under the intoxication of the betel nut. Food is altered, and smell can only endure incense which purifies and exotifies the old, existential stench.

Music? But music is, if anything, that form of expression where the soul is alone with itself, the world left behind, the imagination free to wind in and around itself. It is not a picture or representation of anything; or, following Schopenhauer, it is another world coequal with the old objective one. But the typical music of drugged experience is again unique; like the Indian ragas, it slowly moves along with only the slightest variations, moves interminably like an endless epic narrative and is to Western ears "formless"; in effect, infinite in intent. The finite, dramatic, or classical forms of Western music are experienced as expressing nothing but the rational will and therefore reeking of finite human drives, i.e., the existential and not the eternal. And is the music of drugged experience really "performed"? If so, largely to oneself, with perhaps an audience to overhear it. The drugged ones sing to themselves, even though they are walking down Telegraph Street in Berkeley. The preference for the sliding or the *glissando* is noticeable; definite notes, with their arbitrary pitches, express again the metaphysics which has been abandoned: that which fixes into definite finite entities what is really a *one*, of absolute depth.

It would not be difficult to continue in each of the arts. But our only point was that the imagination, following the lead of, and trying to express an experienced absolute, takes unique forms. That classical art, no matter how it is understood, is also an expression of the absolute, need not be argued here, since it has already been done by Hegel.

And mathematics. Here reason itself is set free to play, create and uncreate systems, all in the domain of "abstraction," a domain which only accidentally has any practical applicability, which no pure mathematician would deign to notice except out of the corner of his eye. It is an intellectual form of pure music, the mind itself now playing with its own inventions, all to express in the realm of thought what the transcendental ego is eternally. But then soon expression is inadequate too. In fact, do not all these expressions still retain an odor of that old life which, purely speaking, the ego knows it is intrinsically beyond? When it bids good-bye to existence forever, it recedes into its own absolute solitude, at which point we the living lose access to it.

If some such thing is the odyssey of the drugged soul in its flight from existence, what meanwhile has happened to existence living its own life? No longer animated by that ego, it first takes on a life of its own, and then finally abandons even that. The radical dissociation of the transcendental ego from existence leaves that existence progressively evacuated of any transcendental meanings; and since it is the very essence of meaning or significance to go beyond or transcend the given, without that animating transcendence, existence itself regresses to absolute presence, a sensory presence without any sense whatsoever. Phenomenologically speaking, the world for the transcendental ego is constituted by that ego, and re-given to that ego as an objective phenomenon. Intentionality, then, is invariably "constitutive." And any ordinary world is constituted in layers, from the simplest perception of things, up through animated things, societies, cultural institutions, and higher orders of meanings up to God. The typical drugged experience reverses this constitution, progressively loses significances, and ends at last with a purely sensory presence. It is that decomposition or regressive deconstitution which *it* calls "mind-expanding." But in fact, it is nothing but a contraction of experience with its infinite mediations and significances, down to the sensory immediate in its pure presence. Since that sensory immediate can disclose no distinctions either in the experienced or between the experiencer and his experience, it is a form of the *one*, and lost within that one, the mind finds itself expanded into an *all* by way of immediacy or intuition. The function of the transcendental ego and its world are reduced to immediacy on both sides, and then collapsed into one. The transcendental ego no longer animates that immediacy with sense, and what is not animated with sense simply is; in their bare being, both are one without distinction.

The progressive de-constitution can be readily illustrated by typical drugged experiences. If phenomenologically or dialectically the most sophisticated constitution is the "other person" and those higher social meanings such as "society" and "state," they are naturally the first to go. Indeed, for their disappearance, it hardly requires more than a fit of disgust or fatigue for the sense of the other as other person to disappear, leaving nothing behind but an irritating presence one would just as soon do without. Under the title "*le regard*," Sartre has given some remarkable analyses of the meaning of the other, which — although Sartre regards them as foundational — might better be taken as descriptive of one modality of the experience of the other: that in which the other appears as a menace to my own freedom, as judge, or that which turns *me* into an object, somewhat like the Medusa. The modality of experience which Sartre describes is already well on its way to a constitutional paranoia, a path taken by certain temperaments soaked with drugs. But if in the first instance the other seems a threat to me, he is still a presence; the spontaneous solution is to obliterate him altogether. He will be as nothing to me. And with this, we have the disappearance of the foundation of either the social or the interpersonal. And, since the profound source of emotional difficulties is precisely the presence of the other, whether social or intimate, this first withdrawal of intentionality is a frequent final solution to the human problem, the "solution" taken by those who choose autism or certain forms of schizophrenia. The drugged experience in itself is but a temporary visit to those realms, which, not surprisingly, can become fixed and residential.

Drugs, then, while frequently taken in company, release the ego from that company for its own self engrossments. They hardly promote sociality, and silence is preferred to conversation — which now is heard as chatter. The vanishing of the other, or his disappearance as another person into a *thing* immediately dries up, as a logical consequence, any empathy, sympathy, or regard for him as a bearer of rights, let alone a focus of either love or hate. All these significances are washed out, and what the drugged one is left with is a something or other of a peculiar form, laughable, odd, a toy with which one can play but need not take seriously. Was it not exactly that seriousness one wished to wash out in the first place? And so the newspaper stories continue on of mothers soaked in LSD, drowning their babies, neglecting them, or finally, the *ne plus ultra*, the Manson "family," a family held together evidently solely by lust, fear, habit, opposition to the world, and the last remaining thread of coherence, obedience to the leader.

If the disappearance of the other, and its correlative, the disappearance of social morality and obligation, is one consequence of the asociality of drugged experience, another correlative is the disappearance of communication. Disorders in writing and speech are familiar: the penmanship runs up and down, words are split anywhere, sentences run on or are never formed in the first place, punctuation is abandoned in favor of dashes, spaces, or nothing at all. In speech, stammering appears, repetitions, wrong words, etc. Now all of this is clear enough when we realize that writing, being later than speech, goes first, and finally speech disappears — not because of some physiological disorder, but because the intent to speak is the intent to communicate; but that presupposes there is another to whom one is speaking and that one has something to say. Since the drugged one has nothing to say, and no one to whom to say it, it is no wonder that he is hardly a master of communication. He will give up in futility. Or if he does not, his preferred communication will be "scat" singing, sounds and rhythms which say nothing, or perhaps he will try to and succeed in speaking in tongues. The dadaists enjoyed all this immensely, and Kurt Schwitters composed an "*Ursonate*," an absolutely meaningless composition delivered with great passion and urgency. But those were delightful adventures of simulation; it's altogether a different matter to *have* to speak meaninglessly. The reduction of speech to its aural expressiveness is its first deprivation of meaning; but then the aural expressiveness may also go, and one is left with grunts and groans. I remember a poet giving a "lecture" consisting of nothing but barking and animal moaning. Perhaps he could have gone even farther.

But the disappearance of the other is hardly the last stage. Even alone in his asocial world, the drugged one may notice certain cognitive functions slipping. As each one fades away, the mind feels more "expanded." The phenomenon of both space and time are radically altered. Both, for normal experience, are possible only through the transcending intentions of an ego which spontaneously so animates them. But now, primordial time is given as an absolute flux. It is now! now! now! To interpret one now as before or after another requires, obviously, a spontaneous comparison; the present *now*! is located in the flux; there were other nows and there will be other nows. The sense, therefore, of time as a flux can only be given through an act of the ego which is not exclusively a part of that flux but is above it, retaining past nows, and expecting future nows. This fundamental power of retention and protention, with their more sophisticated modifications

of memory and expectation, is an intention which transcends
the given now and presents to the self time in its flow — pat-
terns and sequences within time rather than an absolute frag-
mentation into instants. Dramas, melodies, sentences, lives
are within such stretches of time, and impossible within the
instantaneous now. Using the term *memory* for this function
directed to the past, it is not surprising that within the drugged
experience, memory is one the first functions to go. And coevally, expectation and anticipation. In a word, the drugged
one hangs in a perpetual present, without past and without
future. These are not so much denied as simply absent. And
since there are frequently emotional roots of these experiences, what could be less surprising than that certain temperaments torn apart with guilt for their past and dread for
their future look to the annihilation of time for their salvation?
Neither my guilt for what I did or did not do, nor my dread
of an incomprehensible future could take on the slightest sense
if I no longer have the sense of past and future. All that is,
is now. No doubt a grand relief to those suffering from these
passions.

Space, too, undergoes its own particular modification.
For normal perception, space is not in the least an optical
phenomenon of three dimensions. It is the space occupied by
physical bodies, which have their own independent properties, and which conceal sides not immediately given; this space
extends on and on, far beyond my own infinitesimal perception. I am in it, as a fish in water, and I explore what it
contains like a fish in water. Now these transcending meanings are eliminated in one fell swoop by the elimination of
that animating intention of the transcendental ego. Space becomes a *pure given*, that is, an optical phenomenon, and all
its contents, physical bodies, equally are reduced to their purely
phenomenal givenness. They have no meanings beyond, ad-

umbrate nothing, are no longer active bodies within a world not exhausted by them, but become a world on their own, a kind of moving picture without external references. No wonder, then, that in any such "physical world," anything is capable of happening. It instantly becomes what would otherwise look like a magical world; and so we read, again and again, of the drugged ones jumping from ten-story windows, flapping their arms to fly, or running, after their glue-sniffing, straight into an oncoming locomotive. Who knows what happens in their own phenomenological world? In ours, they are killed.

Reasoning suffers its own demise, perhaps earlier than any purely perceptual disorder. For if reasoning is one of the most conspicuously transcending intentionalities, and perhaps one of the very latest acquired, it would be the first to go. Inference of any sort, whether empirical or logical, goes from premises to conclusion in the domain of abstraction. It goes beyond what is given to what must also be or what probably ought to be. To stare at a meaning is hardly to reason either into its premises or its consequences. Reasoning, then, is discursive, hence significant, hence an act of the transcendental ego, although hardly its most appropriate act. But if the transcendental ego is now being considered in its choice of *not* giving meaning, obviously it will not reason, and obviously, the drugged one substitutes for reasoning first mere association, sliding analogies where anything whatsoever can suggest anything else, and indeed, if all is one, why not? André Breton himself said that for the surrealist sensibility, anything whatsoever could be a metaphor for anything else.

If reason or consciousness in any form rests upon some object, the transcending animation of the ego being rejected, it begins to look like intuition. For intuition is distinguished from discursive thought precisely in its immobility; in discursive thought I move from the given to either the not-given or to another given, the movement either a guided one, as in logical thought, or one guided by the very implicit sense of the object itself, as when one perception requires another in order to fill it out or to confirm it. In these discursive acts of thought, it is the very nature of the object to lead me from it to what it itself points to. The resulting thought or experience thereby systematically enriches itself. Or, on the other hand, the discursive or transitional character is unguided, a mere random passage from anything to anything else, the mind attending to a sequence which in and of itself is helter-skelter. The result is a mere assemblage of ideas or impressions, which do not of themselves have any structural connection except that expressed by the word "and": sheer addition. Streams of association, aimless musings, etc. are of this order.

Now intuition, on the contrary, is immobile and non-discursive; it dwells upon its object, is filled with it, and comes to rest in it. It offers to consciousness a beginning; and without intuition, or the intuitive function, the mind would have nothing at all before it. Nothing whatsoever would be given. Now this beginning can also be an end; if the mind can find nothing whatsoever in the intuited to invite it to move on, that is, if the object in and of itself is complete and can, in and of itself, supply no logical motivation to the mind to pass to something else, then that object is in and of itself *absolute*. It is self-contained, dependent upon nothing else, logically derived from nothing else, and therefore presents the character of the absolute. But it must be noted that this character of absoluteness is itself the objective or essential character of the object. Thus, to illustrate with an example not wholly adequate but suggestive, one is objectively motivated upon considering one twin to consider the other, since one twin is in and of itself an absurdity. But one man, in this context, is not, and does not motivate the intuition considering him to consider another man. For such reasons, of course, a man was regarded by Aristotle as a "substance," that which is in and of itself, and not a predicate of another. That this is not wholly true, and that what, in one respect, is a substance, this man, when considered more absolutely, is but a mode of one single and ultimate substance, God, is the burden of Spinoza's argument on the question. Hence for Spinoza, God alone is substance, that alone which can be and be thought in and of itself. The thought is intuitive; and ultimately, for Spinoza, there is only one such thought or intuition which can logically rest upon its object without being objectively or logically motivated to move on to another; that is the thought of God.

In all of this, the decisive question is whether the thought or intuition of something is logically or essentially motivated to move on or whether it simply refuses or simply does not move on. Hence the immobility of thought in its intuitive aspect can have two sources; either there is nothing in its object to demand it to move on, or there is some such thing, but the thought "refuses" or does not move on, even though there are such demands made upon it by the object. In both cases, the thought rests upon its object, and so may be said to be intuitive. But where intuition, in grasping its object, sees that there is nothing forcing it to move on in that object, it sees at the same time that it has the objective truth of that object; or, that it is indeed the adequate idea of its own ideatum. On the other hand, if the ego intuiting refuses to move on when it has before it an object which objectively requires such a movement, then while the thought remains immobile, it is only a pseudo-intuition; "intuitive" since immobile, "pseudo-" because the immobility is subjectively motivated rather than rooted in the nature of the object.

This form of pseudo-intuition is, it seems, the domain of drugged experience. The transcendental ego, refusing to animate intuition or mind, leaves that mind simply staring at its object, fixed upon it. And, even when the object demands completion, that demand is refused. Since the transcending function of the ego has left mind, the mind falls into what is usually called "stupidity," staring at the given in stupor. Sharing one feature, immobility, with genuine intuition, it might be thought to be the same; but then genuine intuition gives itself over to the object and follows its essence, whereas pseudo-intuition refuses the invitation. And since in one case there is no objective reason to move beyond that which presents itself as absolute, pseudo-intuition regards everything it confronts as "absolute," whereas genuine or original intuition must necessarily find only one such absolutely absolute.

Of course, it must be added that absolutely everything does indeed have one abstract side of it which *is* absolute: its being. And consequently, pseudo-intuition is genuine insofar as it merely intuits the being in everything. But to intuit that is to intuit not the specificity of each thing, but only that abstract being which everything manifests and shares. What is lost is precisely that specificity, which is subsequently declared to be unreal.

This is the reappearance, of course, of an old question: How is one to tell pseudo-intuition from genuine intuition? And as so often, Spinoza has been here before and says the essential thing: The true idea is both the measure of itself and of the false. In a word, the true idea, which is adequate to its object, knows that it is adequate and supplies thereby the touchstone for ideas which do not adequately grasp their object, but in their subjective fatigue simply refuse to move on adequately to grasp it.

As the transcendental ego in various degrees and along

various paths bids good-bye to its living function of animating the existence of what supports it, the very organic life of the body begins to deteriorate. Nothing governs it, and far from becoming "natural," it sinks at once into the moribund. Health loses its instinctive zest. Appetite disappears or becomes obsessed with Coca-Cola or lychee nuts. Or ceases to desire anything. Personal hygiene slips, and cleanliness — a concern even of the animals — becomes a matter of indifference. Muscular tone decreases to flabbiness. Laughing and crying, when still present, become sporadic and without appropriate or indeed *any* external occasion. And then there is no laughing or crying at all; a dead indifference is another final solution. The list need not be extended: spatial and temporal disorientation, filth, malnutrition, endless sitting, loss of communication along with the loss of any desire for any relatedness with the world in any of its real forms, and finally vacancy and hospitalization. The transcendental ego has finally abandoned its own existence, and yet either through habit, confusion, or a bad faith which wants to be alive yet not really alive, continues to drag out a simulacrum of life. The body, for its part, has understood the message and is committed wisely to its own destruction; the intoxication and addiction are irreversible and express a decision of the ego made long ago not to animate this body in this situation with significance. It may have taken it a long time to understand its commitment, and it may be shocked when it does, but such was from the beginning its own deepest choice.

Physiological addiction unto death, "incurability," is of course physiological; but it is at the same time a transcendental decision. By "decision," at this point, I mean not so much a question of deliberation, as though the matter were up to an internal debate, with its weighing of issues, and power to opt either way, but rather the following of a resolution resolved by the ego itself. Since the resolution was itself an act of the ego, it was free; and since I now follow it, submit to it, or consent to it, I have only the sentiment of following my own destiny. That some still, at any given point in this entire trajectory of the spirit, try to revolt, try to cure themselves, or try at the last moment to reverse the irreversible, is clear enough; but what it exhibits is a self at odds with itself, either simultaneously or by way of alternation. The irreversibility under discussion is dialectical, not factual. That is, insofar as the ego commits itself to a certain course, the end of that course — if followed — is death in a specific form. But it is impossible to draw an empirical prediction, since in fact the ego remains factually free at any point to reverse itself. This reversal becomes increasingly difficult as the particular course is traversed; more and more has to be reversed or cancelled out; more and more sedimented meanings, phases of life, systems of interpretation and adjustment. And so, as the ego lives through its destiny, it becomes more and more an abstract question whether the reversal is possible. Still, some remarkable cases are known of self-cure among the incurables, none of which, however, qualifies our general thesis that the course of drug addiction is a progressive detachment of the transcendental ego from its vital function of animating its life. It becomes a witness to its own withdrawal, the recession from anything like a world of experience, leaving nothing but a residue of immediate sensation given the significance of being "absolute," and finally the disappearance in death of even that. In its final and more lucid stages, it knows it will not return; the withdrawal from life is irrevocable and, rather than linger, it longs for a final termination of the whole business. Not merely is life too painful, it is more profoundly too senseless to offer the slightest attraction. The ego reverts to itself, finds the perfect source of all sense and clarity, itself with itself, the existential search for clarity finally terminated in a clarity which is the clarity of nothing, the sense of nothing which ever has or ever will exist.

The final stage offers some remarkable resemblances to certain remarks of both mystics and the aged. Practised mystics, such as Ramakrishna, reached the point where it was optional with them whether they "returned to life" or not. Their disciples begged them to return, whereupon they did "out of charity." Boddhisattvas delay their irrevocable ascent into nirvana until the "last man" can be saved. Plato similarly asked why the philosopher who has seen the real sun should ever return to the cave, and gave as a reason the philosopher's own goodness: no one else could possibly rule within the cave so well, but it nevertheless is a form of punishment and not fulfillment. Similarly, the myth of reincarnation presents a return to life as a punishment for having loved it too well; the truly saved never return, or if they do, out of superabundant charity and goodness.

Perhaps it is also not remarkable that the aged, who are not suffering pain, frequently say, in spite of an excellent life, that they would not do it all over again. Once is enough, priceless, fascinating, beautiful, and agonizing, but quite enough.

Appendix II The Ontological Argument in Spinoza

The ontological argument is universally discredited today, generally on logical grounds. It has become a platitude to assert that existence cannot follow from essence, that all analytic propositions are to be interpreted as hypotheses having no existential import. Our platitudes, however, would be falsehoods resting on an inadequate metaphysical analysis for a series of thinkers including Anselm, Descartes, Spinoza, Leibniz, Hegel, and Bradley. At each period the contemporaries of these men raised our objections for us and these objections were not unknown to the philosophers who rested their entire work on the ontological argument. At each period these philosophers insisted that the objections rested on a misunderstanding of precisely what the argument did and did not assert. Such misunderstandings will occur as long as we abstract the ontological argument from its metaphysical context; that is, as long as we alter the significance of the relevant terms. Since this entire context is probably clearest in Spinoza, I should like to reexamine the ontological argument as it occurs there in order to determine whether we are not committing the same errors of misinterpretation as did his contemporaries.

But before a discussion of the ontological argument proper, I should like to clarify the relation of this essay to that argument. I do not intend to "prove" the ontological argument in a direct fashion, since such a procedure would be in direct contradiction to the assertions of the argument. The argument states in some fashion that the existence of God or substance follows from his essence alone; to attempt then to give further grounds for the existence of God than those asserted by the argument would be to destroy that argument. The argument must stand or fall by itself; the only function of this discussion is to elucidate the argument, and not to prove it.

Briefly the argument states that there is an essence whose existence follows necessarily from that essence. That is all. It does not say: I have an idea of such an essence, and therefore God must exist as cause. Nor does it say: there are certain finite things, hence there must be a necessary being as cause. These are both variants of the cosmological argument, and although used by Spinoza, were considered by him to be *a posteriori* and of inferior certitude. Both rest upon a certain empirical fact, the existence of a certain sort of idea or of finite things; and both employ certain notions of causation which we cannot analyze here. But these considerations are irrelevant to the argument in its pure form, which asserts only that there is an essence which necessarily involves existence.

Spinoza does not assert that all essences involve existence, nor that essence as such involves existence. Here he would insist that most essences do not and cannot involve existence. The question concerns only one special essence, the essence of substance, or of that "which is in itself and conceived through itself." This one, Spinoza asserts, must involve existence; and to see why, we must know what Spinoza means by the terms, "essence," "existence," and "substance."

Let us first examine the notion of essence. Essence, for Spinoza, is not a purely logical term, the mere object of any definable sign. Essence expresses something positive, it expresses power or reality. It is certainly not what Santayana for example means by essence, a term wide enough to include square circles, as well as negations of these, etc. "Non-chair" for Santayana is an essence in the same sense as chair, though for Spinoza it would be a mere fiction of the mind, a mere word. From such a conception we could derive no positive properties; we would know only what the thing was not.

"Positive" and "negative," however, are slippery terms, since a word verbally negative may express something positive, as does the word "infinite," for example. Essences cannot be self-contradictory; and since the entire course of nature follows analytically from God who does all that he can do, it follows that there are only essences for those things which were, are, or will be. Anything else must either contradict itself, or contradict what exists. Such unrealizables will be mere fictions of the mind or compositions of words.

Secondly, and more importantly, an essence is not an idea, or a psychological state of some sort. Spinoza distinguishes between the *idea* and the *ideatum*. The idea of a circle would therefore have two aspects: it is, to be sure, an idea, a mode of thought; but it is the idea of a circle which is not a mode of thought, but a determinate mode of extension. The circle is round, and all its radii are equal, whereas it would be absurd to speak of an idea as being round or having radii. Thought and extension have distinct properties, and neither is to be understood in terms of the other. This distinction is clear within the idea; an analysis of the idea itself will exhibit these two aspects. An idea of a house for example is clearly in one sense a psychological act, a mode of thought; but the idea is of something which is made of stone, wood, and bricks, and not ideas. The essence of house or of circle, therefore, neither is nor involves the notion of thought. It is independent of that psychological act which thinks it, and this can be seen within that psychological act itself. This distinguishability of idea and ideatum is essential to the objective and independent validity of thought. A geometer resolves the circle into its proper elements, planes, lines, and the central point; at no point need he mention the thought which is thinking all this. No geometry will be found to posit among its principles ideas as such or anything else psychological. Geometry and logic are sciences independent of psychology, studying objective relations among the things posited.

Not all *ideata* are essences of course. But here we are interested in those *ideata* which are essences and their structural and essential independence from the psychological act by which they are thought. That they are independent can be guaranteed within thought itself simply by the complete analysis of the essence thought of.

These relations hold even when we take as the object of some thought thought itself. If I have the idea of an idea, then the thought which I am thinking of is independent of the particular act of thought by which I think it. Now this should not be understood as asserting that we can think of essences without thinking at all; such would be obviously nonsense, and is asserted by nobody. But it would be asserted that there are aspects within any idea which are logically, structurally, and essentially independent of the act which thinks them, that such a distinction can be demonstrated within thought itself (by the reduction of the particular essence to its principles), and that the independence of any eidetic science from empirical psychology depends upon this distinction.

The conclusion of all this is simply that essences are not ideas, although sometimes ideas are ideas of essences; the essences do not require that particular act of thought for their definition, and hence are structurally independent. This is a first step in the perception of the independence of essence: its independence from mind; it does not yet demonstrate that there are essences which are as a matter of fact existentially independent of everything.

Essences, then, are independent of the psychological act which thinks them; but, considered in themselves, they may be dependent upon other essences, or they may be absolutely independent. The essence of circle depends, among other things, on the essence of plane, of line, etc., since these other essences would figure in its definition. This order of derivation is of course logical, but it is mirrored in the level of existing things: an existing circle depends on an existing plane. The essence of island requires the essence of circumambient water; and so an existing island requires existing circumambient water. The order of essences and things is one and the same. A thing is a mode when it is conceived through another, and the essence of that mode will depend on the essence of that through which it is conceived. And just as the independence of essence from thought is discoverable within thought itself simply by the analysis of the essence, so the dependence or independence of the essence from other essences will be discoverable within thought alone by the adequate analysis of that essence. An independent essence will be one which is conceived through itself and which *is* in itself. These phrases clearly express the same thing: since things will depend existentially upon precisely those things on which their essences will essentially depend, independence of essence is the same as independence of existence. The discernment, therefore, of an essence which is thought through itself will be at the same time the discernment of that which exists through itself; defining the essence is precisely this act of discernment; hence as soon as God or substance is defined as being precisely that essence which is thought through itself, i.e., which is essentially independent, it is seen at the same time that he must exist.

But what kind of existence does such an essence have? Here again we must not import into Spinoza's system conceptions of existence fundamentally foreign to it. For Spinoza there are two sorts of existence: eternity, and duration. Duration is that existence which modes have, and is measured by time; eternity is the existence which independent essences have. When Spinoza speaks of the existence of God he is not attributing to God some sort of surd, some irrational, brute, simply given mode of being; the existence of God, he tells us, is nothing but his essence: they are one and the same thing. To assert God's existence, therefore, is to frame an analytic proposition. One is not adding an extrinsic property to an essence; ultimately the argument is simply the reaffirmation of the absolute independence of God's essence. It is analytic, and therefore requires no additional grounds.

To attribute to God an existence which would add a new determinant to his essence would be to attribute to him the existence appropriate to modes, duration. We cannot know by an analysis of the essence of modes whether they exist or not; we must consult the order of nature which is to say, for finite minds, we must consult experience. Hence to interpret the ontological argument as attempting to prove a synthetic proposition by something like "rational intuition" is to misinterpret it completely. The argument was never anything but an analytic assertion. Whether such a proposition, along with the metaphysics derived from it is held to be "interesting," "fruitful," or "useful" or not depends on what sort of knowledge one is seeking; the ultimate use of such knowledge or any knowledge is a question which more properly falls within ethics, and is a question not neglected, of course, by Spinoza.

The existence of God is therefore his eternity, and his eternity is again the radical independence of his essence. He is substance, and substance is that which is and is conceived through itself. So again we see, now by an explication of the term *existence* that the argument is analytic. But why, it may be asked, do we not end with nothing rather than infinite substance consisting of infinite attributes, each one of which expresses infinite essence? This would be an objection only so long as we forgot Spinoza's conception of essence; it is positive rather than negative, and expresses, therefore, some positive reality, rather than the mere negation of something which would as a matter of fact be nothing but a fiction, and a fiction which more clearly than anything else depended on something else, namely everything else. In a metaphor, substance at this level is like a light shining in a dark space; since the essence in question has already subsumed everything else under it as a modification, there is nothing left which can contradict or oppose it; it is free to expand out infinitely. And as darkness cannot quench light, neither can non-being destroy the being of substance.

The existence of God is thus an eternal subsistence. The existence or duration of modes on the other hand will differ from the eternity of God to the degree that their essence differs from his essence. Since modes are derived essentially, their existence will also be derived, that is to say, they will be dependent upon the rest of the universe; existence does not follow immediately from the essences but only from the existence of their causes, which are, in turn, dependent upon their own causes, etc,; existence for modes will therefore be transitory. Since the existence of a mode cannot follow from its essence, propositions asserting its existence will be synthetic, and experience will be needed by any finite mind in order to ascertain its truth. We can therefore see why existence will be a brute fact, a surd, when it is asserted of modes by finite minds; such properties will be consequences of Spinoza's general conception of the relation between substance and modes. But if we were to begin with existence conceived after the fashion of duration, then clearly we could never arrive at the notion of eternal subsistence. The ontological argument asserting eternal subsistence would then be interpreted after the model of modes, and would always be absurd, a "synthetic" proposition, and wholly undemonstrable. On the other hand, beginning with the notion of an eternal subsistence, one can, if Spinoza is correct, derive a notion of existence or duration which is appropriate to our experiences of finite things.

In terms of this conception of the ontological argument, let us further consider some objections which have been made. The contention has been made, for example, that since the existence of God follows from his essence or definition, anything could be defined into existence, by simply including "existence" in the definition. Thus we might define a hippogriff as a "combined griffin and horse which exists." Would not it then analytically follow that such a creature must exist? The reason that such a being could not exist for Spinoza is not that the combination of horse and griffin violates some supposed rule of nature; such we could not know by reason alone. Rather it is because the combination of these two terms combined with the notion of existence itself contains a contradiction. The first part of the definition, horse and griffin, determines a mode which intrinsically depends on other things, ultimately on the whole circumambient universe; to now assert that such a mode existed in itself would make it independent of that universe. Similarly with the example of the "most perfect island, one of whose perfections is existence." An island is a piece of land surrounded by water. Its essence requires the essence of water, and it existence depends on the existence of the water. To then add that such an island existed in itself would be to contradict what we posited in the first part of the definition. (And if the island had only dependent existence, the point is granted: the island would only exist contingently.) Clearly the same argument would apply to any mode defined into existence. Existence follows only from certain essences, those namely which express infinity, independence, and substance.

Kant, in the portion of the *Critique* devoted to the refutation of the ontological argument, has no trouble disposing of it under the interpretation that it presents a synthetic judgment. But, if it is analytic, he says, then either the conception in your mind is identical with the thing, or else you have given us nothing but a "wretched tautology." Clearly, the argument *is* analytic; that it thereby implies that the thing, God, is identical with your conception has already been disposed of; and that it is a tautology is true, but whether it is "wretched" or not will depend on what value we wish to place on the analytic clarification of existence.

Appendix III The Ontological Argument in Spinoza: Twenty Years Later

The ontological argument has, of course, a long and venerable history; its "refutation" also has a long if not quite so venerable history. No sooner did Anselm formulate it than its "refutation" appeared, and the story is repeated through Descrates, Spinoza, Leibniz, Hegel, Bradley, through our own times. It looks like an argument, hence appeals to logicians; it uses the term "therefore," hence invites a purely formal analysis. But then it may not be an argument at all, and "therefore" may have other uses than the syllogistic. In any case, it would be foolish to formalize what has not been understood; and the understanding of what it says and what it does not say, introduces us at once into those metaphysical systems where it plays a central role. Spinoza was singularly explicit about that context; it therefore might be worth while examining the ontological argument within the context of a system where its meaning might become visible. The argument is here held to be strictly valid, and the career of both it and its refutations to be less that of a recurring malady of human reason itself, than the appearance and disappearance of certain principles of philosophical hermeneutics. If the essence of that argument is an intellectual intuition, is it really a discursive argument? And if it explicitly purports to be true of one unique "entity," God, what claims upon it can be made from a logic which, in its formalization, ignores this decisive difference in content? But before we go into the matter, it should be clear that the function of this discussion cannot be to "prove" the validity of the argument; if the argument is indeed sound, it then requires no additional proof and would be incompatible with any. Our purpose then is strictly interpretive, and no interpretation serves as a premise for what it interprets.

The ontological argument has had a variety of formulations: some speak of a "most perfect being than which nothing more perfect can be conceived," but what is "perfection" and doesn't this version make reference to our capacities? Others speak of a being which "cannot not be," putting it all negatively as if the life of this being consisted in unsuccessfully trying to commit suicide; others call it a "necessary being," suggesting to some that it is necessitated by others, hence contingent upon them; or that being whose "*idea* implies its existence," making the being dependent upon certain contingencies of sentience.

But the subject of the argument in Spinoza's language is God. Substance or *Natura naturans*, all taken as synonymous. It is neither the idea nor the verbal definition of it, although there is such an idea and such a definition. Spinoza defines "substance" as "that which is in itself and must be conceived through itself." At first sight the definition seems a bit too lengthy; obviously nothing which was not in itself *could* be truly conceived through itself, and what has substance got to do with how it must be conceived? Besides, the very sense of "in itself" implies that it is not "in another." But this seems to involve substance itself in negative relations to its own modes, hence logically dependent upon them, a dialectical situation beloved of Hegel. The same would hold of anything whatsoever said about substance; if we declare it to be ontologically "most perfect," we relativize it against the less perfect; if its essence implies its existence, we imply an initial distinguishability of essence and existence only to deny it; if we find it necessary, we envisage it against a domain of pure possibility where it could not be, and thus deny the very sense of the problem. The truth then is that substance is strictly ineffable though equally strictly "conceivable." Everything then which is said about substance has a peculiar sense; it will be the negation of a negation. In a word, the term can only be brought into discursive language, hence made effable, by denying something falsely said of it. Hence the infinite possible versions of the ontological argument. God or substance is not a mere idea, a mere representation, a mere word, a mere possibility, a mere essence, or merely something "better" than hitherto envisaged. Each version raises the possibility of substance being that and denies it. The forms of the "that" which substance is not are as infinite as possible categories of the finite: space, time, relation, causation by another, etc., right on through the very idea of substances, which must be taken in a different sense when applied to substance Itself. Hence all these descriptions must be understood in a pre-eminent sense, through an infinite analogy, when said of that which is called substance. For Spinoza, since substance is the very origin of things, and its idea the source of all intelligibility, that which is this origin and source cannot be really clarified through its own partial effects and modes. On the contrary, good philosophical method demands the opposite; and yet the origin of things, while in itself decisively ineffable, is held by Spinoza to be the subject of an "adequate idea." How indeed can that which is strictly ineffable to discursive language be adequately grasped, to such an extent, that nothing else can be understood except through it?

A few distinctions are in order. Spinoza distinguishes *idea* from *ideatum*; idea is a mode of thinking, ideatum is what the idea is of, which need not be a mode of thinking at all. If I form the idea of a circle, my idea is a thinking about a circle which is not in the least a mode of thinking, but something extended. It has a center and circumference and the radii are equal; none of these properties are true of the idea. But if I should form the idea of an idea, the ideatum would itself be a mode of thinking, like the idea of it. I form an adequate idea of an ideatum, when the idea grasps the ideatum itself, and not a part, aspect, phase, or property of it. How does the idea know that it grasps its ideatum adequately? No external criteria would be relevant, Spinoza explains in the *Emendation of the Understanding*. Truth is a measure of itself and the false, and self-evident truth is found in the initial relation of idea to ideatum. The ideatum, whatever it is, is already something, has, as ideatum, a sense or essence. Now either all of that is grasped by the idea or not; and the idea knows that in the very act of having an ideatum in the first place. Thus if I form the idea of one mode, as given mode it implicates other modes as well as substance, which are not present in the initial idea although implicated by it. I therefore have a self-declared inadequate idea, knowable by the idea itself. Of what could I form an adequate idea? Obviously only of that which is "in itself"; the adequate ideas of other things will relate them back to the primordial in-itself.

What the adequate idea is adequate to, its ideatum, is called substance. Substance itself, then, is the ideatum; the idea has not grasped therefore a "representation" of, an image of, nor a universal concept of substance, but substance itself "in person." Substance is not a universal, substantiality, or deity, but itself a singular, an individual, in the pre-eminent senses mentioned above. But an idea of a singular individual, indeed unique in this case, is an *intuition*, and not a universal concept. Hence the adequate idea in question is an intellectual intuition, precisely that which Kant denied to man but reserved as a possibility to God. For Spinoza, man's idea of God is one and the same as God's idea of Himself; hence the intellectual intuition which is expressed by the ontological argument is the participation by that idea which is the human mind in God considered as thinking of Himself. They are not two ideas which resemble one another, but one and the same.

But if we take a step backwards from this purely immanent or phenomenological analysis of the situation, we might ask how any such thing is possible. The claim is indeed extraordinary although guaranteed by internal analysis. And so we might ask, what is mind such that it can have any such intellectual intuition of substance itself? Mind, says Spinoza, is the idea of the body. And at first sight this would seem to instantly obviate any possibility of an intellectual intuition of substance which is eternal and infinite, and confine the mind's capacities to the sensory on the one hand, and the universal or conceptual on the other. Is not the body a finite mode, inherently dependent upon other physical bodies and their interaction? The modifications in my own body worked by external bodies and forces I am aware of as sensations; the ideas of these sensations are nothing but the ideas of "conclusions without the premises," hence, taken by themselves, inadequate; the premises are of course the infinite concatenation of causes which produced those sensory effects I am aware of. Even my idea of my own body, which constitutes my mind, is inadequate; the body cannot be conceived through itself since it is not through itself but an effect of circumambient nature. Conceptualization from such data of sensation, in terms of their common properties, number, motion, etc., are clearly nothing in themselves, but *entia rationis*, useful but not beings. In such a situation, how could mind form by intellectual intuition the idea of substance itself? Clearly, because our account of the epistemological situation is so far inadequate. The mind is the idea of the body, that is, there is one mode of substance which expresses itself either as body or as its idea, mind. But to suppose the body is an independent thing, finite and merely lost among other finite modes, is to misunderstand the body. The body was never anything but a mode of substance in the first place; and similarly the mind is not absolutely finite, since the absolutely finite is equally a contradiction in terms. Hence on both scores, mind and body, substance is already implicated; body is a mode of substance, its idea, mind, is the same mode thinking, and therefore dependent upon substance. The idea of substance, then, is possible ontologically; whereas a body not the body of substance or a mind which excluded the idea of substance are not possible.

The role of intellectual intuition of substance is, obviously, decisive in any rationalism. The epistemological fear within rationalism is that its adequate or its "clear and distinct" ideas are nothing but that, and in effect that the mind is enclosed within its own objects, its own representations, constructions, or constitutions; that the whole structure of knowledge might be an elaborate fiction, or that it bears nothing but a hypothetical relation to being itself. The problem then is to find if possible that idea which is the idea of something which is, an idea which knows of itself that it is true. At that point, the magic circle of mere representations would be broken, and the ideas of mind would be anchored in reality. Descartes isolated the *cogito ergo sum* as one such anchor; it is a reflective idea, it is not a discursive syllogism, and each time it is enacted, it supplies an intellectual intuition of the being of the very ego thinking it. The ontological argument serves a similar function; the discernment of the idea of substance or God is the discernment of that idea which adequately grasps being, not its image, representation or concept, but substance itself.

The intellectual (or "rational") intuition of substance is the idea of an infinite singular. It is then small wonder that such an object is ineffable; it would share ineffability with all singulars, but now in an infinitely enhanced degree. But "ineffability" conceals some curious reversals of meaning. If nothing drawn from either sense perception or the common notions drawn therefrom can be applied to substance except by way of negating what is already negative in them, it might seem that the idea of substance, far from being adequate, was the least adequate of all, everything said about it being true only by way of infinite analogical remotion. On the other hand, for the rationalists, the exact opposite is the truth; it is not substance which is obscure but everything else commonly taken to be clear on grounds of familiarity as with common notions, or vividness, as with perceptions. *Red* is, measured against substance, a most inadequate idea, no matter how bright it is; and the common conceptions, such as thing or substance, motion, and number, no matter how universally illustrated, remain obscure until seen *sub specie aeternitatis*, that is, from the angle of substance.

Looked at finally, the various versions of the ontological argument all serve the same purpose: to discriminate among things that which is substance. This unique being independently of which nothing else can be or be conceived, has obviously unique properties. Its mode of being is, Spinoza says, eternity and not temporal existence, which he reserves for modes of substance. Its being will be necessary and not contingent upon others. It will be "most perfect" ontologically, absolute and not relative, an "immanent cause" of all other things, and the "cause of itself," hence, we might as well say, "omnipotent." Its "essence implies its necessary being"; only that sort of thing could have necessary being, and necessary being could only hold for that sort of thing. In a word, the essence and being of this being are identical; essence and existence are only distinguishable for modes of substance.

And so, again and again, the various versions of the argument only serve to indicate that what is distinguishable for modes is not for substance. Essence and existence here are the same; cause and effect are the same; and finally the world and its divine principle are the same taken in different ways, *natura naturans, natura naturata.*

But whereas we have no hope of surveying or comprehending the "face of nature," we do have the possibility of an intellectual intuition of its active principle. Substance, then, as the immanent cause of all things, must be, as an idea, the ground of anything claiming to be knowledge. The order of ideas must be the same as the order of things. That idea from which all other true ideas must be deducible "in a geometrical manner" must itself contain the guarantee of its own truth within it. At this point, the ontological argument only indicates that such an idea is true of or adequate to its intended ideatum.

Nothing whatsoever in the ontological argument, purely understood, depends upon premises to the effect that I or someone else actually has such an idea at any given time. Nor can the effect of the argument be to render the being of substance dependent upon our sentience. If no one had such an idea, nothing follows except that no one would know of substance; substance itself timelessly exists, and if finite sentience were obliterated, the only thing that would know of the being of substance would be substance itself, if "knowing" is still the appropriate term. For Spinoza, thought is an attribute of substance, and there is eternally an idea of substance, God's idea of himself. This idea, as we mentioned above, is identical with man's idea of substance. There is but one such idea, a divine idea, which the human mind can participate in. It would carry us too far afield to discuss "ideas," which for us are almost virtually exclusively psychological events, dependent for their actuality upon living organisms, in their older sense an ontological perfection, hence not so much dependent upon brains as rendering anything like a functioning, signifying mind possible.

No doubt at all, some of the misinterpretations of the very sense of the argument arise from suspicions of what might be thought to follow. Is substance a secret surrogate for Jehovah or Christ? Precisely what passion should be poured into the term; or what existential relevance does substance have? But here again Spinoza has responded in advance. The fifth book of the *Ethics* is devoted to man's freedom, a book not sufficiently studied by those who imagine that Spinoza is a "determinist" in a fatalistic sense. The freedom of man consists precisely in the rational intuition of substance. "God's idea of Himself," and the comprehension of Himself and all other things as following from that unique essence-substance in which He participates. The reenactment by man of an infinite thought of an infinite substance may be hopelessly useless for the projects of the *Lebenswelt*, since it is not one of them and could only look like an "escape hatch" to the devotees of Sartre's *engagement*. And yet Spinoza defines it as "blessedness," not a "pleasure," but freedom itself: put otherwise it is for us an act of transcendence, not from one misery to the next, but precisely from the oppressive finality of the *Lebenswelt*, by a reinterpretation of it from the standpoint of a rational intuition of *natura naturans*, another name for the eternally creative substance which cannot not be, and in which we participate.

Appendix IV **What the Mystics Say**

These texts, from various religions, cultures, and times are designed to refresh the reader of an otherwise dry argument with a form of expression which is neither exclusively poetry, religion, nor philosophy, but all three fused into a holy and true beauty. Taken together they may be too rich, but dipped into from time to time, a needed relief, and no doubt at all the best thing in the book. Nothing in them depends upon any strict orthodox theology; but as a continuing song to God from men of many lives, are they not the flesh and blood of both mysticism and metaphysical philosophy? I am much indebted to Thomas Mueller for advice and some labors of selection and assemblage.

India

Looking upon it even from the standpoint of thine own moral and religious duty thou shouldst not waver, for nothing is higher for a warrior than a righteous war.

If thou fallest in battle, thou shalt obtain heaven; if thou conquerest, thou shalt enjoy the earth. Therefore, O son of Kunti, arise and be resolved to fight.

One who is devoted to Yoga, of purified mind, self-subjugated and a master of the senses, realizes his Self as the Self of all beings; though acting he is not tainted.

Noble are all these, but I regard the wise as my very Self; for with soul ever steadfast, he is established in Me alone as his supreme goal.

He who, at the time of death, thinking of Me alone, goes forth, leaving the body, he attains unto my Being. There is no doubt in this.

O son of Pritha, that Supreme Self, in whom all beings abide and by whom all this is pervaded, can be attained by whole-hearted and exclusive devotion to Him.

I am the Way, the Supporter, the Lord, the Witness, the Abode, the Refuge, the Friend, the Origin, the Dissolution, the Resting-Place, the Storehouse and the Eternal Seed.

O Arjuna, I give heat, I sent forth rain and withhold it: I am Immortality and also Death. I am being and non-being the manifested and the unmanifested.

The worshippers of the gods go to the gods: to the ancestors go the ancestor-worshippers: the spirit-worshippers go to the spirits: but My worshippers come unto Me.

Intelligence, wisdom, non-delusion, forgiveness, truth, control of the senses, serenity of the heart, pleasure and pain, birth and death, fear and fearlessness.

Non-injury, equanimity, contentment, austerity, benevolence, fame and infamy: these different states of beings arise from Me alone.

O Gudakesha (Arjuna), I am the Self existing in the heart of all beings. I am the beginning, the middle and also the end of beings.

O Vishnu! swallowing all the worlds with Thy blazing flames, Thou art licking all around. Thy fierce, radiant rays, filling the whole universe, are burning.

Why should they not bow down to Thee, O Mighty Being, O Infinite One, O Lord of the gods, O Abode of the universe, greater than Brahma and even the primeval cause of Brahma; for Thou art the Imperishable; Thou art Existence and Non-existence and all that is beyond.

Fix thy mind on Me alone and rest thine understanding in Me, thus thou shalt doubtlessly live in Me hereafter.

Knowledge is indeed better than blind practice; meditation excels knowledge; surrender of the fruits of action is more esteemed than meditation. Peace immediately follows surrender.

He who hates no creature and is friendly and compassionate to all, who is free from attachment and egotism, equal-minded in pleasure and pain, and forgiving,

Who is ever content and meditative, self-subjugated and possessed with firm conviction, with mind and intellect dedicated to Me, he who is thus devoted to Me is dear to Me.

He who is free from all external dependence, pure, efficient, unattached, undisturbed, and has given up all selfish undertakings, he who is thus full of devotion is dear to Me.

He who neither rejoices, nor hates, nor sorrows, nor desires and who has renounced good and evil, he who is thus full of devotion is dear to Me.

I shall declare now that which is to be known, by knowing which one attains immortality. The Supreme Brahman is beginningless; It is said to be neither existence nor non-existence.

With hands and feet everywhere, with eyes, heads and mouths everywhere and with ears everywhere in the universe, That alone exists enveloping all.

It shines through the functions of all the senses, and yet It is without senses; unattached, yet It sustains all; devoid of qualities, yet It is the experiences of qualities.

It exists within and without all beings; It is unmoving as well as moving, incomprehensible because of Its subtlety; It is far and also near.

Indivisible, yet It exists as if divided in beings; It is to be known as the Sustainer of beings: It destroys and also generates.

It is the Light of lights and is said to be beyond darkness. It is knowledge, the One to be known, and the goal of knowledge, dwelling in the hearts of all.

And he who sees that all actions are being performed by nature alone and that the Self is not acting, he sees truly.

When he sees the separate existence of all beings established in One, and their expansion from that One alone, then he becomes Brahman.

They who thus, by the eyes of wisdom, perceive the distinction between body and Soul, and the liberation of beings from Nature, they attain to the Supreme.

By devotion he knows Me in truth, what and who I am; having thus known Me in truth, he forthwith enters into Me.

From *The Bhagavad Gita*, in *The Wisdom of China and India*, ed. Lin Yutang (New York: Random House, 1942).

The Beginning of Things

The non-existent was not, the existent was not then; air was not, nor the firmament that is beyond. What stirred? Where? Under whose shelter? Was the deep abyss water?

Death was not, immortality was not then; no
distinction was there of night and day. That One breathed,
windless, self-dependent. Other than That there was nought
beyond.

Darkness there was, plunged in darkness in the
beginning; undistinguished water was all this. That which
was, was covered with the void; through the power of heat
was produced the One.

Desire first stirred in it, desire that was the first seed
of spirit. The connection of the existent in the non-existent
the sages found, seeking in their hearts with wisdom.

Their cord was stretched across. Was there a below?
Was there an above? Impregnators there were; powers there
were; will was below; endeavour was above.

Who verily knows? Who will here declare whence this
creation is born, whence it is? On this side are the Gods
through the creation of this universe; who then knows
whence it has come into existence?

Whence this creation has come into existence, whether
he established it or did not, he who is its overseer in the
highest firmament, he verily knows, or he knows not.

From *Vedic Hymns*, trans. Edward J. Thomas (London: John Murray, 1923),
pp. 127-28.

Israel

When I called upon him, the God of my justice heard me:
when I was in distress, thou hast enlarged me. Have mercy
on me: and hear my prayer.

Oh ye sons of men, how long will you be dull of heart?
Why do you love vanity, and seek after lying?

Know ye also that the Lord hath made his holy one
wonderful: the Lord will hear me when I shall cry unto
him.

Save me, O Lord, for there is now no saint: truths are
decayed from among the children of men.

They have spoken vain things every one to his
neighbor: with deceitful lips and with a double heart have
they spoken.

The fool hath said in his heart: There is no God. They
are corrupt, and are become abominable in their ways:
there is none that doth good, no, not one.

The Lord hath looked down from heaven upon the
children of men, to see if there be any that understand and
seek God.

The Lord is my light and my salvation: Whom shall I
fear? The Lord is the protector of my life: Of whom shall I
be afraid?

Whilst the wicked draw near against me, to eat my
flesh.

My enemies that trouble me, have themselves been
weakened, and have fallen.

If armies in camp should stand together against me, my
heart shall not fear.

If a battle should rise up against me, in this will I be
confident.

One thing I have asked of the Lord, this will I seek after: that I may dwell in the house of the Lord all the days of my life.

That I may see the delight of the Lord: and may visit his temple.

The king is not saved by a great army: nor shall the giant be saved by the abundance of his strength.

Behold the eyes of the Lord are on them that fear him: and on them that hope in his mercy.

To deliver their souls from death and feed them in famine.

Our soul waiteth for the Lord: for he is our helper and protector.

Delight in the Lord: and he will give thee the requests of thy heart.

And the enemies of the Lord, presently after they shall be honored and exalted, shall come to nothing and vanish like smoke.

Be still and see that I am God. I will be exalted among the nations, and I will be exalted in the earth.

But to the sinner God hath said: Why dost thou declare my justices, and take my covenant in thy mouth?

Seeing thou hast hated discipline: and hast cast my words behind thee.

If thou didst see a thief thou didst run with him: and with adulterers thou hast been a partaker.

Thy mouth hath abounded with evil: and thy tongue framed deceits.

Sitting thou didst speak against thy brother, and didst lay a scandal against thy mother's son.

These things thou has done, and I was silent.

Thou thoughtest unjustly that I should be like to thee: but I will reprove thee, and set before thy face.

Understand these things, you that forget God: lest he snatch you away, and there be none to deliver you.

Create a clean heart in me, O God: and renew a right spirit within my bowels.

Cast me not away from thy face: and take not thy holy spirit from me.

Restore unto me the joy of thy salvation: and strengthen me with a perfect spirit.

My heart is troubled within me: and the fear of death is fallen upon me.

Fear and trembling are come upon me: and darkness hath covered me.

And I said: Who will give me wings like a dove, and I will fly and be at rest?

Lo, I have gone far off, flying away; and I abode in the wilderness.

I waited for him that hath saved me from pusillanimity of spirit and a storm.

Bloody and deceitful men shall not live out half their days. But I will trust in thee, O Lord.

They shall be scattered abroad to eat: and shall murmur if they be not filled.

But I will sing thy strength: and will extol thy mercy in the morning.

For thou art become my support and my refuge, in the day of my trouble.

Unto thee, O my helper, will I sing, for thou art God my defence: My God, my mercy.

Thus will I bless thee all my life long: and in thy name I will lift up my hands.

Let my soul be filled as with marrow and fatness: and my mouth shall praise thee with joyful lips.

If I have remembered thee upon my bed, I will meditate on thee in the morning: because thou hast been my helper.

And I will rejoice under the covert of thy wings. My soul hath stuck close to thee: thy right hand hath received me.

But they have sought my soul in vain: they shall go into the lower parts of the earth:

They shall be delivered into the hands of the sword: they shall be the portions of foxes.

But the king shall rejoice in God; all they shall be praised that swear by him: because the mouth is stopped of them that speak wicked things.

Save me, O God: for the waters are come in even unto my soul. I stick fast in the mire of the deep: and there is no sure standing. I am come into the depth of the sea: and a tempest hath overwhelmed me.

I have laboured with crying; my jaws are become hoarse: my eyes have failed, whilst I hope in my God.

They are multiplied above the hairs of my head, who hate me without cause.

My enemies are grown strong who have wrongfully persecuted me: then did I pay that which I took not away.

O God, thou knowest my foolishness: and my offences are not hidden from thee:

Let not them be ashamed for me, who look for thee, O Lord, the Lord of hosts.

Let them not be confounded on my account, who seek thee, O God of Israel.

Because for thy sake I have borne reproach: shame hath covered my face.

I am become a stranger to my brethren, and an alien to the sons of my mother.

For the zeal of thy house hath eaten me up: and the reproaches of them that reproached thee are fallen upon me.

And I covered my soul in fasting: and it was made a reproach to me.

And I made haircloth my garment and I became a byword to them.

They that sat in the gate spoke against me: and they that drank wine made me their song.

But as for me, my prayer is to thee, O Lord; for the time of thy good pleasure, O God. In the multitude of thy mercy hear me, in the truth of thy salvation.

That they may not become like their fathers, a perverse and exasperating generation;

A generation that set not their heart aright: and whose spirit was not faithful to God.

And their days were consumed in vanity, and their years in haste.

How lovely are thy tabernacles, O Lord of hosts: My soul longeth and fainteth for the courts of the Lord.

My heart and my flesh have rejoiced in the living God.

For the Sparrow hath found herself a house, and the turtle a nest for herself where she may lay her young ones:

Thy altars, O Lord of hosts: My king and my God.

Mercy and truth have met each other: justice and peace have kissed.

The mountains melted like wax, at the presence of the Lord: at the presence of the Lord of all the earth.

The heavens declared his justice: and all people saw his glory.

Knew ye that the Lord he is God: he made us, and not we ourselves.

I will sing to the Lord as long as I live: I will sing praise to my God while I have my being.

Let my speech be acceptable to him: but I will take delight in the Lord.

From the Psalms in *The Holy Bible*, Douay Version.

Arabia

Of the people there are some who say:
We believe in God and the Last Day;
But they do not really believe.

In their hearts is a disease;
And God has increased their disease:
And grievous is the penalty they incur.
Because they are false to themselves.

When they meet those who believe,
They say: We believe;
But when they are alone
with their evil ones,
They say: We are really with you:
We were only jesting.

And say not of those
Who are slain in the Way
of God: They are dead.
Nay, they are living,
Though ye perceive it not.

And your God
Is one God;
There is no God
But he,
Most Gracious,
Most Merciful.

God will not
Call you to account
For thoughtlessness
In your oaths,

But for the intention
In your hearts;
And He is
Oft-forgiving
Most Forbearing.

God! There is no god
But he, — the Living,
The Self-subsisting, Eternal.
No slumber can seize him
Nor sleep. His are all things
In the heavens and on earth.
Who is there can intercede
In His presence except
As He permitteth? He knoweth
What appeareth to His creatures
As Before or After
Or Behind them.
Nor shall they compass
Aught of His knowledge
Except as He willeth.
His throne doth extend
Over the heavens
And the earth, and He feeleth
No fatigue in guarding
and preserving them
For He is the Most High,
The Supreme (in glory).

Let there be no compulsion
In religion: Truth stands out
Clear from Error: whoever
Rejects Evil and believes
In God hath grasped

The most trustworthy
Hand-hold, that never breaks.
And God heareth
And knoweth all things.

And the likeness of those
Who spend their substance,
Seeking to please God
And to strengthen their souls,
Is as a garden, high
And fertile: heavy rain
Falls on it but makes it yield
A double increase
Of harvest, and if it receives not
Heavy rain, light moisture
Sufficeth it. God seeth well
Whatever ye do.

He granteth wisdom
To whom He pleaseth;
And he to whom wisdom
Is granted receiveth
Indeed a benefit overflowing;
But none will grasp the Message
But men of understanding.

Ah! ye are those
Who love them,
But they love you not, —
Though ye believe
In the whole of the Book.
When they meet you,
They say, We believe:
But when they are alone,

They bite off the very tips
Of their fingers at you
In their rage. Say:
Perish in your rage;
God knoweth well
All the secrets of the heart.

Nor can a soul die
Except by God's leave,
The term being fixed
As by writing. If any
Do desire a reward
In this life, We shall give it
To him; and if any do desire
A reward in the Hereafter,
We shall give it to him.
And swiftly shall We reward
Those that serve us with gratitude.

But what hath come
To these people,
That they fail
To understand
A single fact?

They may hide
Their crimes from men,
But they cannot hide
Them from God, seeing that
He is in their midst
When they plot by night.

Who can be better in religion than one
Who submits his whole self
To God, does good,

And follows the way
Of Abraham the true in faith?
For God did take
Abraham for a friend.

If it were His Will,
He could destroy you,
O mankind, and create
Another race: for He
Hath power to do this.

Say: Will ye worship,
Besides God, something
Which hath no power either
To harm or benefit you?
But God, — He it is
That heareth and knoweth
All things.

With Him are the keys
Of the Unseen, the treasures
That none knoweth but He.
He knoweth whatever there is
On the earth and in the sea.
Not a leaf doth fall
But with His knowledge:
There is not a grain
In the darkness
Of the earth, nor anything
Green or withered,
But is inscribed in a Record
Clear.

Leave alone those
Who take their religion

To be mere play
And amusement,
And are deceived
By the life of this world.
But proclaim to them
This: that every soul
Delivers itself to ruin
By its own acts.

Who can be more wicked
Than one who inventeth
A lie against God . . . ?

No vision can grasp Him,
But His grasp is over
All vision: He is
Above all comprehension,
Yet is acquainted with all things.

To God do belong
The secrets
Of the heavens and the earth,
And to Him goeth back
Every affair for decision:
Then worship Him,
And put thy trust in Him:
And thy Lord is not
Unmindful of aught
That ye do.

But celebrate the praises
Of they Lord, and be of those
Who prostrate themselves
In adoration.

And serve thy Lord
Until there come unto thee
The Hour that is Certain.

But those who were blind
In this world, will be
Blind in the Hereafter,
And most astray
From the Path.

All faces shall be humbled
Before Him — the Living,
The Self-Subsisting, Eternal:
Hopeless indeed will be
The man that carries
Iniquity on his back.

This is so, because God
Is the Reality: it is He
Who gives life to the dead,
And it is He Who has
Power over all things.

God is the light
Of the heavens and the earth.
The parable of His Light
Is as if there were a Niche
And within it a Lamp:
The lamp enclosed in Glass:
The glass as it were
A brilliant star:
Lit from a blessed Tree,
An Olive, neither of the East
Nor of the West,
Whose Oil is well-nigh

Luminous,
Though fire scarce touched it:
Light upon Light!
God doth guide
Whom He will
To His Light:
God doth set forth Parables
For men: and God
Doth know all things.

Say: The Angel of Death,
Put in charge of you,
Will duly take your souls:
Then shall ye be brought
Back to your Lord.

If God were to punish
Men according to what
They deserve, He would not
Leave on the back
Of the earth a single
Living creature: but He
Gives them respite
For a stated Term:
When their Term expires,
Verily God has in His sight
All His servants.

It is He Who gives Life
And Death; and when He
Decides upon an affair,
He says to it, Be,
And it is.

It is not fitting
For a man that God
Should speak to him
Except by inspiration,
Or from behind a veil,
Or by the sending
Of a Messenger
To reveal, with God's permission,
What God wills: for He
Is Most High, Most wise.

Verily in the heavens
And the earth, are Signs
For those who believe.

The life of this world
Is but play and amusement:
And if ye believe
And guard against evil,
He will grant you
Your recompense, and will not
Ask you to give up
Your possessions.

It was We Who
Created man, and We know
What dark suggestions his soul
Makes to him: for We
Are nearer to him
Than his jugular vein.

The Judgment ever approaching
Draws nigh:
No soul but God
Can lay it bare.

Do ye then wonder
At this recital?
And will ye laugh
And not weep, —
Wasting your time
In vanities?
But fall ye down in prostration
To God, and adore Him!

He is the First
And the Last,
The Evident
And the Immanent:
And He has full knowledge
Of all things.

Nor misfortune can happen
On earth or in your souls
But is recorded in
A decree before We bring
It into existence:
That is truly easy for God:
In order that ye may
Not despair over matters
That pass you by,
Nor exult over favors
Bestowed upon you.
For God loveth not
Any vainglorious boaster, —
Such persons as are
Covetous and commend
Covetousness to men.
And if any turn back

From God's Way, verily
God is free of all needs,
Worthy of all praise.

God is He, than Whom
There is no other god; —
The Sovereign, the Holy One,
The Source of Peace and Perfection,
The Guardian of Faith,
The Preserver of Safety,
The Exalted in Might,
The Irresistible, the Supreme:
Glory to God!
High is He
Above the partners
They attribute to Him.

He is God, the Creator,
The Evolver,
The Bestower of Forms.
To Him belong
The Most Beautiful Names:
Whatever is in
The heavens and on earth,
Doth declare
His Praises and Glory:
And He is the Exalted
In Might, the Wise.

And whether ye hide
Your word or publish it,
He certainly has full knowledge,
Of the secrets of all hearts.
Should He not know, —

He that created?
And He is the One
That understands the finest
Mysteries and is
Well-acquainted with them.

Ah! would that Death
Had made an end of me!
Of no profit to me
Has been my wealth!
My Power has
Perished from me! . . .
So no friend hath he
Here this Day.

They see the Day indeed
As the far-off event:
But We see it
Quite near.

And exalted is the Majesty
Of our Lord: He has
Taken neither a wife
Nor a son.

And we pried into
The secrets of heaven:
But we found it filled
With stern guards
And flaming fires.

And round about them
Will serve youths
Of perpetual freshness:

If thou seest them,
Thou wouldst think them
Scattered Pearls.

When the World on High
Is unveiled;
When the Blazing Fire
Is kindled to fierce heat
And when the Garden
Is brought near; —
Then shall each soul know
What it has put forward.

Again, what will explain
To thee what the Day
of Judgment is?
It will be the Day
When no soul shall have
Power to do aught
For another:
For the command, that Day
Will be wholly with God.

It is the Star
Of piercing brightness; —
There is no soul but has
A protector over it.

So he who gives
In Charity and fears God,
And in all sincerity
Testifies to the Best, —
We will indeed
Make smooth for him
The path to Bliss.

But he who is
A greedy miser
And thinks himself
Self-sufficient,
And gives the lie
To the Best, —
We will indeed
Make smooth for him
The Path to Misery;
Nor will his wealth
Profit him when he
Falls headlong.

We have indeed revealed
This Message
In the Night of Power:
And what will explain
To thee what the Night
Of Power is?
The Night of Power
Is better than
A thousand Months.
Therein come down
The angels and the Spirit
By God's permission,
On every errand:
Peace! . . . This
Until the rise of Morn!

By the Token of
Time
Verily Man
Is in loss,
Except such as have Faith,

And do righteous deeds,
And join together
In the mutual teaching
Of Truth and of
Patience and Constancy.

Say: He is God,
The One and Only;
God, the Eternal, Absolute;
He begetteth not,
Nor is He begotten;
And there is none
Like unto Him.

From *The Holy Qur-an*, Translation and Commentary by Abdullah Yusuf
Ali, three volumes, Shaikh Muhammad Ashraf, Lahore, no publication
date.

Persia

A human being is not a human being while his tendencies include self-indulgence, covetousness, temper and attacking other people.

A disciple had asked permission to take part in the 'dance' of the Sufis. The Sheikh said: 'Fast completely for three days. Then have luscious dishes cooked. If you then prefer the "dance", you may take part in it.'

Assuredly there is a price on this knowledge. It is to be given only to those who can keep it and not lose it.

You possess only whatever will not be lost in a shipwreck.

None learned the art of archery from me
Who did not make me, in the end, the target.

The sanctuary is in front of you and the thief is behind you.
If you go on, you will win; if you sleep, you die.

Throughout the long night a man wept
At the bedside of a sick man.
When day dawned the visitor was dead —
And the patient was alive.

A beggar went to a door, asking for something to be given to him. The owner answered, and said: "I am sorry, but there is nobody in." "I don't want anybody," said the beggar, "I want food".

The rose has gone from the garden; what shall we do with the thorns?

Do not speak of your heartache — for He is speaking.
Do not seek Him — for He is seeking.

What can I do Muslims? I do not know myself.
I am no Christian, no Jew, no Magian, no Musulman.
Not of the East, not of the West. Not of the land, not of the
sea.
Not of the Mine of Nature, not of the circling heavens,
Not of earth, not of water, not of air, not of fire;
Not of the throne, not of the ground, of existence, of being;
Not of India, China, Bulgaria, Saqseen;
Not of the kingdom of the Iraqs, or of Khorasan;
Not of this world or the next: of heaven or hell;
Not of Adam, Eve, the gardens of Paradise or Eden;
My place placeless, my trace traceless.
Neither body nor soul: all is the life of my Beloved . . .

To your mind, I am mad.
To my mind, you are all sane.
So I pray to increase my madness
And to increase your sanity.
    My 'madness' is from the power of Love;
    Your sanity is from the strength of unawareness.

One went to the door of the Beloved and knocked. A voice
asked: 'Who is there?'
    He answered: 'It is I.'
    The voice said: 'There is no room here for me and thee.'
The door was shut.
    After a year of solitude and deprivation this man
returned to the door of the Beloved. He knocked.
    A voice from within asked: 'Who is there?'
    The man said: 'It is Thou.'
    The door was opened for him.

Salih of Qazwin taught his disciples:
   'Whoever knocks at the door continually, it will be opened to him.'
Rabia, hearing him one day, said:
   'How long will you say: "It will be opened"? The door has never been shut.'

'Being' is absolutely good.
If it contains any evil, it is not Being.

When someone knocked on the door, Bayazid called out:
   'Whom do you seek?'
   The caller answered:
   'Bayazid.'
   Bayazid replied:
   'I, too, have been seeking "Bayazid" for three decades, and I have not yet found him.'
We wrote a hundred letters, and you did not write an answer.
   This, too, is a reply.

I saw a guard hitting a dog with a stick.
   The dog was howling as it suffered the strokes.
   I said: 'O dog, why has he struck you?'
   He said: 'He cannot bear to see one better than himself.'

From *The Way of the Sufi* by Idries Shah. Copyright © 1968 by Idries Shah. Reprinted by permission of E. P. Dutton.

Who seeketh Me findeth Me
Who findeth Me knoweth Me
Who knoweth Me loveth Me
Who loveth Me, I love
Whom I love, I slay

Whom I slay, I must requite
Whom I must requite, Myself am the
Requital

Quote from a Sacred Tradition attributed to Ali the Divine, extracted from *Sufi: Expressions of the Mystic Quest* by Laleh Bakhtiar (1976). Reprinted by permission of Thames and Hudson Ltd., London.

Germany

Furthermore, since God cannot be distracted by the numbers of things, neither can the person, for he is one in One, in which all divided things are gathered up to unity and there undifferentiated.

There never was another such union (as between the soul and God), for the soul is nearer to God than it is to the body which makes us human. It is more intimate with him than a drop of water put into a vat of wine, for that would still be water and wine; but here, one is changed into the other so that no creature could ever again detect a difference between them.

Goodness is neither made, created nor engendered but itself is the begetter, the procreator of the good; and the good, to the extent that it is good, is not made or created, but is born as if it were the child or son of goodness.

He refers to that something in man which is of God's order, which has nothing in common with anything else, and by which man is of the genus and species of God.

I also say that in God there is neither sorrow, nor crying, nor any pain.

I have spoken heretofore of emptiness, that is, of innocence, to the effect that the more innocent and poor the soul is, the less it has to do with creatures, the emptier of things that are not God, the more surely it takes to God, gets into him and is made One with him, itself becoming God. Then, to use St. Paul's words, the soul sees God face to face and no longer as an idea or image.

He will suffer because he likes to suffer for God and to bear
God's will and he thus ends in being God's Son,
transformed by God into God.

. . . for the foundation of spiritual blessing is this: that the
soul look at God without anything between; here it receives
its being and life and draws its essence from the core of
God, unconscious of the knowing-process, or love or
anything else.

. . . for nature begins its work with lowliest things, whereas
God begins with those things that are most perfect. Nature
makes the man from the child, and the hen from the egg,
but God makes the man and then the child, the hen and
then the egg. Nature first makes the wood warm, then hot,
and only then gives the wood over to fire, but God begins
by giving creatures existence. That is where time comes in,
and all the properties of things which belong to time —
existing beside the timeless. So, too, God gives out the Holy
Spirit, before the gifts of the Holy Spirit.

. . . One to one, one from One, one in One and the One in
one, eternally.

The heat and the essence of fire are two different things, far
apart in nature, yet close together in space and time. So,
too, God's sight and mine are far different — utterly
dissimilar. . . .

Let us take first the text: "Out of the silence, a secret word
was spoken to me." Ah, Sir! — What is this silence and
where is that word to be spoken? We shall say, as I have
heretofore, it is spoken in the purest element of the soul, in
the soul's most exalted place, in the core, yes, in the essence
of the soul. The central silence is there, where no creature

may enter, nor any idea, and there the soul neither thinks nor acts, nor entertains any idea, either of itself or of anything else.

Whatever the soul does, it does through agents. It understands by means of intelligence. If it remembers, it does so by means of memory. If it is to love, the will must be used and thus it acts always through agents and not within its own essence. Its results are achieved through an intermediary. The power of sight can be effectuated only through the eyes, for otherwise the soul has no means of vision. It is the same with the other senses. They are effectuated through intermediaries.

In Being, however, there is no action and, therefore, there is none in the soul's essence. The soul's agents, by which it acts, are derived from the core of the soul. In that core is the central silence, the pure peace, and abode of the heavenly birth, the place for this event: this utterance of God's word. By nature the core of the soul is sensitive to nothing but the divine Being, unmediated. Here God enters the soul with all he has and not in part. He enters the soul through its core and nothing may touch that core except God himself.

But an idea, so received, necessarily comes in from outside, through the senses. Thus the soul knows about everything but itself. There is an authority who says that the soul can neither conceive nor admit any idea of itself. Thus it knows about everything else but has no self-knowledge, for ideas always enter through the senses and therefore the soul cannot get an idea of itself. Of nothing does the soul know so little as it knows of itself, for lack of means. And that indicates that within itself the soul is free, innocent of all instrumentalities and ideas, and that is why

God can unite with it, he, too, being pure and without idea or likeness.

Higher than these are the angels who work with fewer instruments and also with fewer ideas. The highest seraph has only one. He comprehends as unity all that his inferiors see as a manifold. But God needs no idea at all, nor has he any.

God has perfect insight into himself and knows himself up and down, through and through, not by ideas, but of himself. God begets his Son through the true unity of the divine nature. See! This is the way: he begets his Son in the core of the soul and is made One with it. There is no other way. If an idea were interposed, there could be no true unity. Man's whole blessedness lies in that unity.

Now you might say: "Naturally! But there is nothing to the soul but ideas." No! Not at all! If that were so, the soul could never be blessed, for even God cannot make a creature in which a perfect blessing is found. Otherwise, God himself would not be the highest blessing, or the best of ends, as it is his nature and will to be — the beginning and the end of everything. A blessing is not a creature nor is it perfection, for perfection (that is, in all virtues) is the consequence of the perfecting of life, and for that you must get into the essence, the core of the soul, so that God's undifferentiated essence may reach you there, without the interposition of any idea. No idea represents or signifies itself. It always points to something else, of which it is the symbol. And since man has no ideas, except those abstracted from external things through the senses, he cannot be blessed by an idea.

"Where is he that is born king of the Jews?" Now let us
see where this birth takes place. It takes place, as I have
so often said before, in the soul, exactly as it does in
eternity and with no difference, for it is the same birth and
occurs in the essence, the core of the soul.

This raises questions. Granted that God is Mind in all
things and is more intimate to each than anything is to
itself . . .

If the soul had known God as perfectly as do the
angels, it would never have entered the body. If the soul
could have known God without the world, the world would
never have been created. The world, therefore, was made
for the soul's sake . . .

I want to say one thing which may mean two or three
different things to you. But understand me rightly! The
intellect that peers into and penetrates all the corners of the
Godhead sees the Son in the Father's heart and puts him
at its own core. Intellect that presses on that far is not
content with goodness, nor with wisdom, nor the truth, no,
nor even with God Himself. To tell the truth, it is no more
content with the idea of God than it would be with a stone
or a tree. It can never rest until it gets to the core of the
matter, crashing through to that which is beyond the idea of
God and truth, until it reaches the *in principio*, the
beginning of beginnings, the origin or source of all goodness
and truth. The intellect's sister, the will, is well satisfied
with God as goodness, but the intellect disdains all that
and pierces to the root of the matter, to the source of the
Son, from whom the Holy Spirit blossoms. That we all may
understand this and eternally be blessed by it, may the
Father, the Son, and the Holy Spirit help us. Amen.

Why did God become man? So that I might be born to
be God — yes — identically God.

From *Meister Eckhart: A Modern Translation* by Raymond Bernard Blakney (New York: Harper & Row, 1941). Reprinted by permission of the publisher.

But that which is in part, or the imperfect, is that which
has its source in, or has sprung from, the Perfect.

The partial things can be apprehended, recognized, and
expressed; but the Perfect cannot be apprehended,
recognized, or expressed by any creature in the measure of
its creaturehood. Therefore we call the Perfect "Nothing,"
for it is not of the nature of creatures, therefore the creature
as creature cannot recognize nor apprehend it, name nor
conceive it.

Beside it, or without it, there is no true Essence! That
which has flowed out from it, is no true Essence and has
no Essence except in the Perfect, but is an accident, a
brightness, or a visible appearance, which is no Essence,
and has not Essence except in the Fire whence the
brightness flows out, as in the case of the sun or a candle.

Sin is nought else, but that the creature turns away from
the unchangeable Good and betakes itself to the changeable;
that is to say, that it turns away from the Perfect to that
which is in part and imperfect, and most often to itself. . . .
What did the Devil do else? What as his going astray and
his fall else, but that he presumed to be also somewhat,
and would have it that somewhat was his, and somewhat
was due to him? This presumption, and his I and Me and

Mine, these were his going astray and his fall. And thus is he to this day.

But how shall my fall be amended? It must be amended as Adam's fall was amended, and in the selfsame way! By whom, and in what way was that amendment brought to pass? Mark this: Man could not be without God, and God could not without man. Wherefore God took human nature, or manhood, upon himself and was made man, and man was made God. Thus was the amendment brought to pass.

And in this renewal and amendment, I can, may, and shall do nothing of myself, but simply let it come to pass, in such fashion that God alone may do and perform all things in me, and I may suffer Him and all his workings and his divine will. But because I will not suffer this, but am wholly possessed by my own existence as "I," "Mine," "Me," and the like, God is hindered . . . For this cause my fall and my going astray remain unamended. Behold! all this comes of my arrogating something to myself.

. . . if our inward man were to make a leap and spring into the Perfect, we should find and feel how immeasureably, numberlessly, and endlessly noble and better the Perfect is than all that is imperfect and partial, and the Eternal above the temporal or perishable, and the fountain and source above all that flows or can ever flow from it . . . whosoever will have the one must let the other go. For no man can serve two masters.

Therefore, although it be good and profitable that we should ask and learn and know what good and holy men have wrought and suffered, and likewise how God has willed and wrought in and through them, yet were it a thousand times better that we should in ourselves learn and

perceive and understand, who we are, how and what our
life is, what God is in us and works in us, what He will
have from us, and to what ends He will or will not make
use of us. For, wholly to know oneself in the truth is above
all meaning: it is the highest learning; if you know yourself
well, you are better and more praiseworthy before God,
than if you did not know yourself, but knew the course of
the heavens and of all the planets and stars, the virtue of
all herbs, and the bodily and intellectual frame of all
mankind, the nature of all beasts, and had further all the
arts of all who are in heaven and on earth. For it is said,
there came a voice from heaven, saying, "Man, know
thyself." Therefore there is this saying too: "Never was
there a going out so good but that an indwelling had not
been far better."

For blessedness lies not in much and manifoldness, but in
One and oneness. And in short, blessedness lies not in any
creature or working of the creatures, but it lies alone in
God and in His working. Therefore should I wait only on
God and His work, and let go all creatures with their
works, and first of all myself. And all the works and
wonders that God has ever wrought or shall ever work in
or through all creatures, yea, God Himself with all the good
that is His — so far as these things exist or are done outside
of me, they can never make me blessed. But only insofar
as they exist and are done in me, are loved, known, tasted,
and felt in me.

For a true lover loves God, or the Eternal Good, alike in
having and in not having, in sweetness and in bitterness, in
joy and sorrow; for he seeks alone the glory of God and of
that which is God's, and he seeks it neither in spiritual
nor natural things, and therefore he stands alike unshaken

in all things, at all seasons. Hereby let every man judge
how he stands toward God, his Creator and Lord.

Now be assured that no one can be enlightened unless
he has first cleansed and purified and freed himself. And
further, no one can be united with God unless he has first
been enlightened.

A man should stand and be so free from himself, that
is, from selfhood, I-hood, Me, Mine, and the like, that in all
things he should no more seek and regard himself and his
own than if he did not exist, and should take as little
account of himself as if he were not and another had done
all his works.

Behold now, all disobedience is against God, and nothing
else. In truth, no creature or creature's work, nor any thing
that we can name or think of, is against God or displeasing
to Him; nothing is against God but only disobedience and
the disobedient man; in short: All that is, is well-pleasing
and agreeable to God, saving only the disobedient man; he
is so displeasing and hateful to God and grieves Him so
sore, that, if it were possible, a man would suffer a
hundred deaths, and suffer them all willingly, for one
disobedient man, in order that but in one man disobedience
might be slain and his obedience be born again.

Of a truth we ought to know and believe that there is
no life so precious and good and well pleasing to God, as
the life of Christ, and yet, to nature and selfhood, it is the
bitterest life. The careless and free life, on the contrary,
is the sweetest and pleasantest life to nature and selfhood
and I-hood. But it is not the best; and in many men it may
become the worst.

But it is quite otherwise where there is spiritual poorness and true humility. And this comes from finding and knowing in truth how man, of himself and his own, is nothing, has nothing, can do and is capable of nothing, but only infirmity, evil, and wickedness . . . And therefore there is nothing that he may demand, but from the humility of his heart he says: "It is just and reasonable that God and all creatures should be against me, and have claims to me and against me, and that I should not be against any one nor have any claims." Hence it follows that the man may not and will not crave or beg for anything, either from God or the creatures, beyond mere needful things, and for these only with shamefacedness, as a favor and not as a right. . . . For he has no rights in respect to anyone, and therefore he thinks himself unworthy of anything.

Moreover, when a man has this poor and humble spirit, he comes to understand aright, how all men are bent upon themselves, and inclined to evil and sin, and that on this account it is needful and profitable that there be order and rules, law and precepts, to the end that the blindness and foolishness of men may be corrected, and that vice and wickedness may be kept under and constrained to conformity; for otherwise, men would be much more mischievous and ungovernable than dogs and cattle.

Nothing burns in hell but self-will. . . . For a man's Best would be and is, that he should neither seek nor love himself nor his own in anything, neither in things spiritual nor things natural, but should seek and love only the praise and glory of God and His divine will.

. . . for all things have their essence more truly in God than in themselves. . . .

Where God is man, or where He dwells in a deified man, nothing is complained of but sin, and nothing else is grievous; for all that is, and is done, without sin, is as God will have it and is His. But mourning and sorrow for sin must and ought to continue in a deified man until his bodily death, even should he live till the Day of Judgment, or forever. From this cause arose that secret anguish of Christ of which none can tell or knows save himself alone, and therefore it is called and is, a mystery.

Now mark! The True Light is God or divine, but the False Light is nature or natural.

And as God and the True Life are without all I-hood, selfhood, and self-seeking, so to nature and the natural and false Light belong the I, the Me, the Mine, and the like, so that in all things that Light seeks itself and its own ends, rather than pure Good. This is its property, and the property of every natural thing. Now mark how it is deceived from the very outset. It does not wish nor choose the Good simply, and for the sake of the Good, but wishes and chooses itself and its own as the Best, and this is false and is the first deception.

In short: All that can be deceived, must be deceived by this False Light.

And now since this False Light is nature, it possesses the property of nature, which is to intend and seek itself and its own in all things, and what may be most expedient, easy, and pleasant to nature and itself. And because it is deceived in this, it imagines and proclaims it to be most proper that each should seek and do what is best for himself. . . . Further, this False Light says that it has got beyond conscience, and that whatever it does is well done.

Therefore he who is without conscience is either Christ or the Devil.

He who will suffer God, must suffer all in the One, and in no wise resist any suffering. But this is to be Christ. He who resists suffering and refuses to endure it, will not and cannot suffer God. That is to say: We may not withstand any creature or thing by force or fighting, either in will or works. But we may indeed without sin prevent affliction, or avoid it and evade it.

But what is Paradise? All things that are; for all that is, is good and joyous. Therefore it is called a Paradise, and is so indeed. It is said also that Paradise is an outer court of Heaven. Even so all that is, is verily an outer court of the Eternal and Eternity, and especially what we may recognize and know of God and Eternity, in time and in temporal things and in creatures. For the creatures are a guide and a way to God and to Eternity. Thus all this is an outer court or forecourt of Eternity; and therefore it may well be called a Paradise, and be so in truth.

Were there not this self-will, this will of the creature's own, there were likewise no property, nothing owned. In Heaven there is nothing owned, wherefore in Heaven there reigns content, true peace, and all bliss. Were there one in Heaven who presumed to own aught, he would instantly be cast out into Hell, and would become a devil.

He who has or will or wishes aught of his own, is himself owned, and he who has and wills naught of his own, and desires to have naught, is quit and free and owned of naught.

By the Father, I understand the Perfect, Simple Good, which is All and above All, and without which and besides which there is no true Essence nor true Good, and without which no good work ever was or will be done. And in that it is All, it must be in All and above All. And it cannot be anyone of those things which the creature, as creature, can comprehend and understand . . . Therefore we name it also "Nothing"; meaning thereby that It is none of all the things which the creature can comprehend, know, conceive, or name, in virtue of its creature-nature.

And thus the man comes wholly to poorness, and indeed he becomes naught to himself and in him becomes naught all that is somewhat, that is, all created things. Such is the first beginning of his true inward life; and thereafter, God himself becomes the man, so that nothing is left which is not God or of God, and nothing is left which arrogates anything to itself. . . . On this wise we should attain to a true inward life. And what then further befalls, what is revealed to us, and what our life is thence-forward none can rhyme or write. It has never been uttered by man's lips, nor has it entered into the heart of man to conceive, the manner thereof in truth.

And our witness is Christ, who declares: "He that will enter otherwise than through me, comes not in, nor comes to the highest truth, but is a thief and a murderer." A thief, for he robs God of His honor and glory, which belong to God alone; he arrogates them to himself, and seeks and purposes himself. He is a murderer, for he slays his own soul, and takes away her life, which is God Himself. For as the body lives by the soul, even so the soul lives by God. Moreover, he murders all those who follow him, by his doctrine and example.

Spain

A great thing it is that the soul which has scaled the
heights of contemplation, being still in mortal flesh, may be
caught up so as to behold God in His Essence, without
use of the senses, as St. Paul affirms of himself. And this,
as St. Thomas says, is a state midway between that of the
blessed in Heaven and of those who live here below on
earth. But although this be so, let us hear the counsel of
Solomon. 'Hast thou found honey, brother? Eat so much as
is sufficient for thee, lest thou be filled therewith and vomit
it.'

. . . the searcher into the Divine Majesty shall be crushed
and overwhelmed by the great glory of God. This theology
is better or more perfect than the first, . . . for it uses the
first as a beginning, and as steps whereby it may climb the
ladder of love.

The first theology God teaches in order that we may
contemplate Him as the highest Truth, while this of which
we speak, presupposing the other, which it takes as proved,
passes to the love of Him as the highest Good.

. . . for it is based upon the deep and profound heart of
man, which is dark indeed, — that is, deprived of human
understanding, so that the Spirit of God may come upon its
darkness, and the waters of its desires, and say: 'Let there
be light' . . .
Furthermore it is called the coming of the Lord to the
soul, for by its means the Lord visits His own who with
sighing call upon Him.

. . . it is the kingdom of God which we must gain by
conquest and by art, since we have it within us, and every

day also we pray for it: it is a royal priesthood, whereby,
when we are masters of ourselves, we may offer ourselves
to God; it is a deep hush made in the Heaven of our souls,
brief though it be and not lasting as the righteous man
desires; it is a service which we do to God alone, adoring
His Majesty only; it is a seat which we have made ready for
Him that He may abide in the heart of our being; it is a
tent which the traveller pitches in the desert; it is our most
strong tower of refuge whence we may spy out heavenly
things; a golden vessel wherein we lay up the manna in the
ark of our inmost selves; it is a valley in which the richest
wheat abounds; it is a victory which conquers the lesser
world, subjecting it wholly to God; it is a vineyard to be
tended with vigilance, and the shade that we greatly long
for, where we taste of its fruit; it is the unction from the
Holy One, which teaches all things; it is a garden enclosed
on all sides, whose key is given to God alone, that He may
enter whensoever He will.

   With burning acid gold is refined, and when the dross
is removed it comes from the crucible refulgent. Let us have
shame that we are so cold in an emprise so great as that
of pleasing God. Ah, did we but feel true shame we should
take courage to shed our blood for Him that we might be
the lovelier in His sight. . . .

For if God created the whale, He created also the frog . . .

The joys of the world are carnal, vile, deceptive, brief and
transitory. They are won with labour, held with anxiety,
and lost with grief. They endure but a little, yet the harm
they do is great. . . .

   The beginner must think of himself as of one setting
out to make from a barren piece of ground, full of weeds, a

garden in which the Lord may take His delight. His Majesty
uproots the weeds, and will set good plants in their place.
Let us then suppose that this has already happened, — that
a soul has determined to live the life of prayer, and has
already begun it. With God's help, we have, like good
gardeners, to make these plants grow, and water them with
care so that they die not, but rather produce flowers which
shall give out great fragrance and so afford refreshment
to our Lord. So may He come often to this garden to delight
Himself therein and take His pleasure among these virtues.

Why should the soul call 'dark night' that divine light
which, as we say, illumines it and purges it of its
ignorances? To this the reply is that for two reasons the
divine wisdom is not only night and darkness to the soul
but also pain and torment. The first is the height of divine
wisdom, which exceeds all the capacity of the soul, and
to it is therefore darkness. The second is the meanness and
impurity of the soul, for which cause the wisdom of God
is painful and afflictive to it, besides being dark.

For this cause St. Dionysius and other mystical
theologians call this infused comtemplation a 'ray of
darkness' — , that is, to the soul not yet enlightened and
purified, — for by its great supernatural light it conquers the
natural power of the reason, and deprives it of its natural
means of understanding . . . And this is the cause why,
when God descends from Himself to the soul not yet
transformed, this illuminating ray of His secret wisdom
causes thick darkness in the understanding.

The second manner of the soul's sufferings arises from
its natural and spiritual weakness: for, when this divine
contemplation strikes it with a certain force, in order to

strengthen and subdue it, it suffers so greatly in its
weakness that it all but faints.

. . . God Himself is to the soul as many lamps, because she
has the knowledge of each of them, and each in its own
way gives out heat of love; all of them unite to form one
simple essence, and all of them are as one lamp, which
lamp is all the lamps, because it gives light and burns in all
ways.

A great and a dreadful miracle — yea, a miracle of the
devil — is it that men should cease from loving their God
and not journey ever towards Him with power and
swiftness, as to their very Centre, being stayed at times by
obstacles no greater than straws, at other times by
obstacles that are none. Who would not wonder at seeing
an immense rock suspended and hanging in the air with
nothing impeding its course? And how much greater a
wonder is it to see a soul created by God suspended in the
air of vanity, its course stayed by so slight a straw as a
question of 'honor' or some such worldly interest, being for
this deprived of its highest Good.

Oh, divine Centre! Oh, infinite Good that art of infinite
attraction! What is it that restrains me from seeking Thee?
What is it that stays my path? What that delays my course?

St. Augustine the Great and the most modern writers speak
of it as the soul's 'depth', because it is the most interior
and secret place of all, where no images of created things
may enter, but only . . . that of the Creator. The deepest
hush and the deepest silence are here, for no form of
created thing can reach this centre, and in respect of it we
are godlike or divine, — so like, indeed, to God Himself that
wisdom calls us gods. This empty, void, and formless state

of intimacy is raised above all created things, above all feelings and powers of the soul; it transcends all time and place, and the soul remains in perpetual union and unity with God, Who is its beginning.

. . . the thing which is first and chiefly loved gives name, nature and form to the will which loves. Whence it is to be concluded that since the property of love is to absorb, convert and transform the lover into the Beloved or into the thing loved, if the will love chiefly things of the earth, it becomes as earth; earthly it becomes and earthly is its love; and if it love mortal things, mortal and human is its will; if it love angels, it becomes angelic; if it love Thee, our Lord and God, it becomes divine.

So then, just as a cloud which is penetrated by the force and brightness of the sun's rays, filled and (if the word be allowable here) saturated with light, is itself like the sun, however it be looked at; just so, when Christ unites, not only His virtue and light, but His very Body and Spirit, with the faithful and just, and in some sort mingles His very Soul with their souls, and His Body with their bodies, in the way I have described, Christ looks out from their eyes, speaks from their tongues, works through their senses; their faces, their countenances, their movements are Christ, Who thus occupies them wholly. So intimately does He take possession of them that, though His Nature in no way destroys or corrupts their own, there will be nothing seen in them at the Last Day, nor will any nature be found in them other than His Nature.

Indeed, it is like the union of matrimony, but so much the stronger and more excellent as the rite is the straiter and more pure. It is purer than betrothal or marriage after the

flesh; and even so, or more, does it excel such marriage
in the intimacy of its union. For whereas in the one there is
defilement of the body, in the other there is deification both
of soul and flesh. Here there is mutual affection between
the wills of two persons; there all is one will and one
desire. Here the body of the one is master of the other;
there, without destruction of her substance, Christ the
Spouse transforms His Bride into His own Body, in the
manner aforesaid. Here, men often stray; there, they walk
ever securely.

The birth of the soul of Christ signifies properly that
the stain of sin, which made the soul in form like to the
devil, is taken away, and that we receive the grace and
righteousness so that we are fashioned after His likeness.
But the birth of Christ in us is not only that the gift of
grace comes to the soul, but that Christ's very Spirit comes
and is united with it, — nay, is infused throughout its being,
as though He were soul of its soul indeed. And thus,
infused and absorbed by the soul, this Spirit takes a
possession of its faculties and powers, not fleetingly nor in
haste, nor merely for a short time as happens in the glories
of contemplation and in the raptures of the spirit, but
abidingly, and with a settled peace, in like manner as the
soul reposes in the body. And Christ Himself says of it
thus: 'He that loveth Me shall be loved of My Father, and
We will come unto him, and make Our abode in him.'

So entirely is the soul overwhelmed with superfluity of
sweetness that the overplus passes to others. Whence these
seasons of enlightment and graces, or this union in
sweetness of the soul with Christ in prayer, has something
in it of the lightning flash: I mean that its brilliance is
quickly over. For our powers and feelings, while this mortal

life endures, are of necessity compelled to busy themselves
with other thoughts and cares, without which man lives
not, nor can live.

But in Christ's presence as revealed to the faithful in
prayer, when He gives them inspiration and joy, the greater
part of the soul and its powers are at rest, and He alone
works secretly in them repose and blessings which cannot
be described.

Christ is born in us whensoever we fall to considering
our lives, when we see and abhor their wretchedness and
confusion, when we meditate on the wrath of God which
we have deserved, and when in our grief and our desire to
appease Him, we turn with faith, love and contrition, to the
mercy of God and the ransom wrought by Christ. It is then
that Christ is born within our souls.

And we say that He is born in us because then His
very spirit enters our soul; He becomes its familiar friend,
works in it His grace, which is, as it were, a ray or a
refulgence of His Presence, takes up His abode in the soul
and makes it beautiful. And thus it is that Christ begins to
live in the soul; namely, when He begins to work in and
through it the works proper to Himself, for the most sure
and certain signs of life are works.

For, if we consider the secret things that come to pass
within ourselves, we shall find that this order and harmony
among the stars, as we contemplate it, brings rest to our
souls; that, as our eyes are fixed intently upon the heavens,
our desires and troubled affections, which surged
tumultously in our breast by day, are gradually lulled to
rest, we know not how; and that, sinking, as it were, to
sleep, these desires are calmed, restored to their rightful

place, and brought imperceptibly into subjection and due order. We shall find, too, that, as they are humbled and stilled, the reason, which is chief and lord of the soul, rises above the rest, recovers its right and strength, and, as if inspired by this glorious heavenly vision, conceived high thoughts, which are worth of itself, and in some sort mindful of its first beginning, sets all that is mean and vile in its proper place, and tramples it underfoot. Thus, with reason enthroned once more as empress of the soul, and its other parts reduced to their fit rank, the whole man is in an ordered and peaceful state.

But what of ourselves, who are reasonable beings? The rude and insensible works of creation, the elements, — the earth, the air — the animals, order themselves, and go to rest, when the sun sets and the resplendent host of heaven appears. See you not how silence is now over all things, as though they gazed in this most beauteous mirror, and forthwith were composed and at peace, returning to their places and offices, and contented with them?

Without any doubt peace is that good part which is in all things everywhere: wherever men see it they love it.

From *Spanish Mysticism: A Preliminary Survey* by E. Allison Peers (London: Methuen & Co. Ltd., 1924). Reprinted by permission of the publisher.

Appendix V **A Retrospect**

To those readers who have followed my previous writings, perhaps a brief note is in order. *Objectivity, The Autobiographical Consciousness*, and the present work form together a trio not altogether unknown to students of nineteenth century idealism, but which at first sight might seem to be a hopeless contradiction. There may be indeed any number of contradictions in a series of works written from 1956 to 1978; and yet this note is intended as something of a mollification of some appearance of hopeless incoherence. In these three works there has never been anything but an effort to address what I dearly hope is something not too remote from the absolute or God as far as I can see it. Needless to say, the whole matter has nothing whatsoever to do with anything clerical, creedal, ritualistic, or anything else not strictly philosophical. And yet, "philosophical" means so many things; I hope it is not exclusively defined by its contemporary servants in their infatuation with a finite logic, a finite epistemology, a finite ethics or aesthetics. But enough has been said about that already.

In any event, *Objectivity* was written to defend the objectivity of the phenomenological object; it is whatever it is exactly as it presents itself to attentive and critical consciousness; to open one's ontology to all that presents itself, or all that one encounters through any mode of consciousness, is seriously to open one's mind to a range of being rarely recognized today. *Objectivity* defends this absolute range of being, which of course terminates in the idea of absolute being, or God, and refuses any limitations thereof on any but phenomenological grounds. It ends with the name of God as *absolute object*.

A second work, *The Autobiographical Consciousness*, looks at what was omitted, but not denied, in the first work. Who am I? Am I to be excluded or ignored from my own philosophy? Well, so much the worse for both me and my philosophy. The introduction of the first-personal singular as a philosophical interest of that very first-person singular sets the theme of that work. But the "I" is caught in an ironical or paradoxical situation; it is both transcendental as well as existent.

Existence is not itself the name for essence or eternity; on the contrary, it names a domain of being which is wholly and essentially accidental. It is happening, chance, accident, and for us a synonym for life. The life in life, its zest, love, tragedies, and ecstasies — all are flowers of chance, but a chance which happens to the eternal transcendental ego or self. This second book looks into some of these human passions, passions to and for the eternal ego, and seeks within each one that frightful and magnificent paradox of the living self. It looks at the life of an *absolute subject*.

This present third member of the trio looks at the identity of the transcendental ego or self with God Himself; they are identical in themselves, and therefore the identity of mysticism and any truly rational philosophy.

In all of this, there are not three disparate ideas, but merely one and the same, turned over from three standpoints.

Another book, *Public Sorrows and Private Pleasures*, looks at certain recent and yet repetitive phenomena of the ethical-political order, in order to trace dialectically their demise as ideologies. Each has its reason, and each has its reason for self-destruction. A second part of the work looks away from all ideologies in order to define in four different ways a philosophical subjectivity, which aims at no political power whatsoever, but only at long last to be with itself and its God. But such also was the beginning of this small venture.

About the Author

William Earle, Professor of Philosophy at Northwestern University, is author of *Objectivity, The Autobiographical Consciousness, Public Sorrows and Private Pleasures*, and co-author of *Christianity and Existentialism*, as well as numerous articles which have appeared in *Ethics, Review of Metaphysics, Journal of Philosophy* and other journals. Aside from teaching at Northwestern University, he has been a visiting lecturer at Harvard, Yale, and Stanford Universities.

DATE DUE